THE MAN WHO FELL TO EARTH

©2016 S. Fabian Butalla

Published by Hellgate Press

(An imprint of L&R Publishing, LLC)

Hellgate Press
PO Box 3531
Ashland, OR 97520
email: info@hellgatepress.com

Interior & Cover Design: L. Redding

Cataloging In Publication Data is available from the publisher upon request.

Printed and bound in the United States of America
First edition 10 9 8 7 6 5 4 3 2 1

This book is dedicated to
Robert Gordon Givens and his family,
to Eleanor and Louis J. Fabian…and to
Derek Olson, Erika Kneen, Janice Wallake,
Karen Silverwood, and Jack for their support.

CONTENTS

THE MAN WHO FELL TO EARTH

The Incredible
True Story of
WWII Flyboy
Robert Givens

S. Fabian Butalla

Preface

THE UNITED STATES VETERANS OF WORLD WAR II were young when the call to duty arose. Many were drafted into military service. Others felt compelled to join the fight for freedom as volunteers against the unprovoked attack by Japan on the American forces at Pearl Harbor and the atrocities of Adolph Hitler's Nazi regime. Thus the world was at war on fronts both east and west of the United States from 1939 to 1945.

Bob Givens was eighteen years old when he opted to join the Air Corps, and he was both proud and anxious to serve his country. He was sent to the European Theater of Operation as a top turret gunner on a B-17. Surviving a fall from his plane as it broke apart and his subsequent landing in the North Sea was nothing short of miraculous. A variety of people and events that impacted him in his early life gave Bob the determination, skills, and confidence to overcome nearly-certain death then and at several other times throughout his long life.

The majority of surviving World War II veterans are over ninety years old, or have passed away, and their stories have gone with them in most cases. I was privileged to interview

Bob Givens, who was eighty-nine years old at the time, as he gladly shared his life story with me. It is an honor to have been able to preserve it, not only for his family, but for posterity as well.

Home on the Range

WINTERS IN NORTHERN MINNESOTA ARE OFTEN notoriously harsh. As heavy snow bundled up the small village of Leonidas and all exposed drops of liquid transformed into crystalline hardness, 1933 was no exception to the norm. The townspeople waited for the fluffy whiteness to stop falling. Then the shovels would emerge from garages, basements, and porches where they had become home to dust bunnies and spiders over the past several months. The cleanup would begin like an on-time parade. Up and down the streets, most of the men, some women, and a few of the older children donned every piece of warm clothing they possessed and shovels in hand, they literally "put their backs into it" as they cleared sidewalks, driveways, and ice-skating rinks.

As soon as they were able to leave their yards, children appeared, looking like walking cocoons as nearly every inch of their bodies was muffled and wrapped. With wooden sleds in tow, they were heading for the sliding hill on the edge of town. Some, with skates slung over their shoulders and a hockey stick or a broom in hand, forged their way to the local ice rink.

In the basement of one of the homes, on such a winter night, a group of young boys was chatting with one another as each of them was focused on the project at hand. While every one of them enjoyed sledding and ice skating, they were all committed to being exactly where they were at that time. It was a meeting of an exclusive number of eight-to-ten-year-old boys who shared an interest in making model airplanes. They had trudged through the deep snow in places where the shovels had not yet touched. The parents of one boy named Ed had agreed to allow his friends to come to their home periodically and they offered their basement as a place for them to congregate. A large table in the middle of the room with an overhead light provided just what was needed for the boys to work on their individual creations.

In the early 1930s, a model airplane kit could be purchased at the local dime store for ten-to-twenty-five cents. Most of the boys earned the money by doing chores such as piling wood, shoveling sidewalks, or mowing grass in the summer. Each boy purchased his own kit and brought it to Ed's house for assembly, which could take several days to complete. While some kits may have included the same type of plane, the way they were painted or finished off distinguished each one from the others.

As the boys opened their kits, studied the directions, and laid out the pieces, one lad's thoughts lead him further than the parts on the table before him. His mind took him beyond the rock walls of that basement as he imagined himself actually lifting off the ground, and flying through the air. Often wondering how birds were able to achieve flight, he was even more fascinated with the flying machines of the day. Young Bob Givens pictured himself in one of those planes and tried to visualize what it must be like to experience the power of flight.

Most of the boys seemed less fixated on the idea of actually flying in a plane someday. Rather, they loved the camaraderie of the airplane club and their finished models which they could then play with or display on a shelf at home. However, over the years, Bob's thoughts and dreams were often filled with wishful longings of flight.

As numbered pieces of balsa wood were removed from a kit, careful study was given by each boy to the plan for assembling his new plane. In order to protect the plan, wax paper was placed between it and the thin sheets of balsa wood. The fuselage, wings, struts, and props all had to be carefully cut out and then glued together. There was also a paper in the box which was stamped with outlines of the ribs and certain other parts of the plane. These also had to be cut from balsa and glued to the plane. Then came the paint, and each boy thoughtfully chose his colors. Finally, the kits contained a certain type of clear paper that had to be placed around the model and pulled as firmly as possible. When it was sprayed with water, the clear wrap tightened around the plane and gave it a shiny finish. It all took time and patience. Some of the boys had more experience in making models than the others and they would willingly lend a helping hand. It was always a time of happiness for these boys, and in later years, Bob would admit, "It kept us out of trouble."

Born on January 21, 1924 at the Moore Hospital in Eveleth, Minnesota, Bob was the only child of Laura and George Gordon Givens. Their home was in the adjacent mining village of Leonidas, which was named after the prospector Leonidas Merritt, who first discovered iron ore in that area. It was part of the great Minnesota Iron Range, that produced massive amounts of pure red ore which was removed from open pits and subterranean mines all over that part of the state for more than one hundred years.

George Givens had worked in the copper mines of Michigan and he served as an engineer with the Rainbow Division of the Army during World War I, building bridges across France. When he returned to Michigan after his military service, he married a girl named Laura Brown. They had heard about the boom on Minnesota's Iron Range and the need for workers, especially those who spoke English. So George and Laura moved to Leonidas where he worked as a stationary engineer (elevator operator) for the Oliver Mining Company, hoisting and lowering men, timber, and ore at the underground mine nearby, while his wife worked as a telephone operator.

Laura Givens was completely devoted to her son and she did everything she could to raise him properly. As the years passed, and no other children were born to them, little "Rob," as she often called him, became all the more precious to her. He was not allowed out of their yard without one of his parents until he was five years old. One day when several of

Bob's parents, Laura and George Givens.

the neighborhood children were running up and down the street playing tag, Bob decided to test the limits of his mother's cautious restrictions by lifting his foot to put it on the fence. Out the front door flew Laura Givens, brandishing a fly swatter, with which she smacked the seat of his pants. She didn't have to do it again. He had learned his lesson, and he respected her for it.

"She was just, I guess, so close to me that she didn't want anything to happen to me," reminisced Bob many years later. "It did me good later on."

Not sure how much education his father had, Bob was nonetheless aware that his mother had only gone through the sixth grade. However, she was an excellent cook. Her meatloaf was better than steak, as far as Bob was concerned, and he devoured her wonderful vegetable/meat pies called "Pasties." Laura kept an immaculate house, which was her castle. She knew how to set a perfect table. Somehow, Laura had learned a lot about manners, which she taught to young Bob from the time he was four years old. Bob's mother instructed him in no uncertain terms that adults outside of their family were never to be addressed by their first names, but always by "Mr., Mrs., or Miss" followed by their last names.

Many years later, Bob freely admitted that although his dad never said much, he was a good provider, and Bob always knew that both of his parents loved him very much. Bob never heard them argue. "They got along perfectly. It was beautiful. I had the best mother and father any boy in this world could dream of," he said with a wistful smile.

Things didn't always go so smoothly for young Bob, however. His mother, in her desire to keep her young son clean and well-dressed, distinguished him from many of the neighborhood children, and he was bullied because of it. Believing he was spoiled due to the fact that he was an only child, and because of the nice, clean clothes he wore, Bob got called "Sissy" by some of the village boys. Most of those bullies wore torn overalls and dirty, worn-out boots. Bob learned to fight his way out of it on several occasions until there was no more "Sissy."

Bob had grown taller than most of the boys in his class by the time he reached sixth grade. That year, he was asked to play Santa Claus for the kindergarten and young elementary students at the school. Bob was pleased to take on the role. Because his parents were so good to him, he had always believed in Santa himself, but he was taunted because of it. However, he had learned to deal with bullies before, and they didn't tease him for long.

Ice skating was one of the favorite pastimes of young people on the Iron Range, many of whom went on to gain fame as Olympians and professional hockey players. The large Eveleth "Hippodrome" was built to house an indoor skating area. On Saturdays, this arena had open skating, and since it was enclosed, for many it was a very welcome change from being outside in frigid temperatures. The Hippodrome was only a couple of miles from the Givens' home in Leonidas. Bob and his friends would often enjoy it on Saturdays as they grew up.

As luck would have it, there was a small outdoor ice rink directly across the street from Bob's house. The village maintained it, flooding it as soon as the temperature dropped below freezing in October. Young Bob and the neighborhood kids could skate there almost any day they wished throughout the winter.

Bob loved to go to the ice rink to play hockey. For boys like Bob, it was something to look forward to after school on long winter days. He could put on his skates at home and run over to the rink, where he and many others would skate

Bob playing hockey at the ice rink
across the street from his home.

until after dark. At 6:00 p.m., the front door of his house would open and his mother would call at the top of her lungs, "Rob, 'Jack Armstrong' is on!"

Bob would race across the street, remove his skates with practiced swiftness, and head straight for the kitchen. A primary form of entertainment for many families in those days was the radio. It provided music, news, and gripping, suspense-filled stories, which were most often broadcast in episodes. "Jack Armstrong" was Bob's favorite, and he tried to never miss one of Jack's adventures. Another program that fascinated Bob was "Jimmy Allen," which was about a pilot. These stories had some fighting and a lot of action, and they kept Bob glued to the radio, hanging on every word. His imagination was in high gear as he visualized all of the characters who were speaking and every scenario that engulfed them.

****

The 4th of July was a time of celebration in most of the small towns across the Iron Range. Each year, George Givens would purchase a large bag of fireworks. Bob would run from house to house and tell all of the neighbors when the display would begin. Soon after dark, from the backyard of the Givens' home, skyrockets were lit. They traveled high into the air with a final burst of sparkling, colorful grandeur, much to the delight of everyone in the neighborhood.

Fishing was a pastime that Bob enjoyed with his dad occasionally, but they didn't have a boat. A neighbor named Ole had a nice wooden rowboat and two sons, one who was older and one younger than Bob. Once in a while, Ole's boys didn't want to go, so Ole would ask Bob to fish with him. He had a trailer for the boat and they would haul it over to Wynne Lake near Giant's Ridge or to Kendall Lake near Leonidas. Ole taught him how to make bobbers out of cedar with a bead on top. Then they would paint them.

****

Bob's birthday was always a big event at his house, and his mother would have a nice party for him. She would be busy for hours in the kitchen before the guests arrived. Besides family members, Bob was allowed to invite some of his friends from school. Every year, they would all enjoy the same special cake that his mother made. It was a three-layer Devil's Food cake with lemon-custard filling, and Bob couldn't get enough of it.

****

At the age of eight, Bob joined the Boy Scouts and was officially dubbed a "Tenderfoot." Over the next eight years, he learned several skills that would serve him well in the future; most notably, swimming.

With a paddle in hand, he learned to navigate a canoe away from the shore, then dump the canoe. He was taught to swim under the overturned canoe and take a few breaths in the air space there in order to survive. He then swam back out, flipped the canoe, got back in, and paddled to shore. He was very proud of himself, knowing he could do this.

At the Chicagami Scout Camp a few miles south of Eveleth, there was an annual diving competition. After much practice, Bob achieved a high level of confidence and at the age of fifteen, he won an award for best diver, of which he also took much pride.

Bullying doesn't end with elementary school by any means, and Bob encountered it again at the Chicagami Camp with the Boy Scouts when he was in his teens. One boy was antagonizing several others including Bob by taunting them, using scare tactics and serious verbal threats. After deliberating about the situation, the boys approached the Scout Master. They described their dilemma and he listened thoughtfully. This man was an assistant football coach during the school season.

"How many of you are there?"he asked. "Can't fifteen or twenty of you take care of one bully?"

The bunkhouses were screen enclosures with canvas sides. The Scout Master suggested a plan. "When he's in bed, lift the canvas on his side and throw a bucket of water on him."

They did just as he had advised them, and it worked. The bully stopped threatening others and he became a star football player on the team that won the Iron Range Football Conference title that year. Bob was also on that team.

So it was that young Bob learned about comradeship and the skills of being together and getting along with others during his years in the Boy Scouts. He gave that organization the utmost credit for instilling in him confidence in the water. He overcame fright and shock, and the experiences of going out into the lake to swim while at camp removed fear of the water from him. He had learned to love swimming.

During their formative years, some children are fortunate in having parents who encourage and make possible the exploration of a variety of skills. George and Laura Givens provided many opportunities for their son to engage in sports and other activities. His mother always said to Bob, "Whatever you do, try to do it well." Thus began his introduction to music.

While his piano lessons with the teacher at the Leonidas School did not last long, Bob next tried the clarinet, which he played for several years. There was a village band in Leonidas and Bob joined it. When he was in ninth grade, he marched in a parade with the band and for doing so, he was paid a few dollars by the village.

This was a moment of decision for Bob, but he didn't have

to think long before he was sure how he wanted to spend that money. Mounting his bicycle, he pedaled the five miles from Leonidas to the airport in the town of Virginia, where he hoped to get a ride in a real airplane. As he rode toward the runway, perspiring and out of breath, he saw a man just getting into a plane. Bob laid his bike down and ran toward the J3 Cub, in which the pilot sat ahead of a single passenger seat in a closed cockpit.

"Mister, please! Could you take me for a ride? Please?" he begged. "I can give you three dollars!"

Well, three dollars was a good amount of money back then, so the man replied, "Okay, come on, kid. I'll give you a ride."

It was Bob's first ride in an airplane, and it sure didn't disappoint him. He climbed into the back seat, more excited than he had ever been. As the engine revved up and the propeller began to rotate first slowly, then so fast you couldn't see the blades any longer, Bob's heart raced almost as quickly. The pilot guided the plane toward the runway and drove it like an automobile out to the end. Then he shouted to Bob, "Hold on kid!" They started slowly rolling down the runway. Before he knew it, they were racing down that runway, faster than Bob had ever traveled before. The liftoff was a moment of sheer euphoria for a young boy with dreams of flying.

The view was amazing as they cruised up over the towns of Virginia, Eveleth, and Leonidas. From the perspective of a bird, Bob gained a new insight into the area where he lived. His eyes were bulging and his mouth was agape at the sight of houses, buildings, mines, and roads, all surrounded by trees and lakes. It was definitely a dream-come-true for the young boy.

The following year, Bob heard about someone giving rides again at the Virginia airport. His mother was going to visit her sister in that town and Bob asked to go along. From his aunt's house, he hitched a ride out to the airport and got to fly on a Ford tri-motor aircraft. It was a "big deal." The more Bob rode in planes, the more he wanted to do it.

****

A boy named Wilbur was Bob's best friend from 4th grade through high school. He and Wilbur got along great. They never had a fight and just enjoyed shooting marbles, hunting, and sharing secrets. During the summer they would often hitchhike out to nearby Ely Lake to go swimming. Playing Monopoly was also a favorite pastime for the two boys. They would spend hours purchasing property and building houses and hotels with the fake money.

While in junior high and high school, Bob played several sports including basketball, football, and hockey. He was on the Pee Wee hockey championship team that beat Eveleth in 1936, which was reason to celebrate. However, basketball was his favorite sport and in the tenth grade he was a starter on the Leonidas team. Being involved in all of these sports had taught him to work with others as a team.

Between the love and devotion of his parents, the deep friendships he had formed, and the skills he was learning in the Boy Scouts and sports, Bob was growing up and forming his own personality. All of these things would play a significant role in his life as time went by.

From the age of ten to fifteen, Bob's friendships with the boys in the airplane club deepened. Sometimes Ed's dad would ask him to do chores like pulling dandelions from the lawn. So Bob and the others would all pitch in to pull the yellow pests and help Ed get it done so they could get back to the basement as soon as possible. When nothing but green was visible in the yard, they hustled into the house and scrambled down the stairs. It was always a competition to see who could get his model done first, yet there was never an argument or fight among those boys.

Sometimes this same group would play hide and seek, marbles, tag, football, hockey, broomball, or shooting rubber band guns in the woods. In the back of Ed's house was a hayfield, where the boys made a little airfield for their model airplanes. After using the old hand mower to cut through the tall grass and weeds, the boys plotted out their runway. Rubber bands were used to crank up the propellers on their planes. After many, many twists of a drill that had a hook on the end of it, the planes were released – and they would fly!

Nearby there stood an old water tower that rose 100-150 feet. More than once, the boys would climb the ladder to the top of that tower, light one of their model airplanes with a match, and watch it go down in flames. It was exciting to be that high off the ground and to watch the model plane ignite, only to become a ball of fire which fortunately burned itself out before it hit the ground. With youthful disregard for their safety, the boys cheered the plane's descent. None of their parents was aware of these dangerous exploits, and it may have remained a secret until now.

****

Laura Givens had three sisters who lived nearby. At Thanksgiving and Christmas, their families, including five of

Young "Rob" with his mom and dad.

Bob's cousins would come to the Givens house to enjoy the holiday meal.

The enticing aroma of savory meat cooking was mingled with the sweet scent of recently-baked pies or cakes as the guests entered the home. Bob enjoyed the company of his cousins and playing with them.

One summer day, Bob and his parents put on their best clothes and headed over to the nearby park at Ely Lake. Bob's five cousins were there and his aunts and uncles as well, and all were dressed in their finest. It was a special occasion as they had all agreed to hire a professional photographer for a family picture. Everyone took their place in the group. The photographer assisted them in lining up and several photos were taken of Bob's family that day. Lowering his head, Bob said, "They're all gone now but me — I'm a survivor."

****

Three Christmases in a row, George Givens bought his son a gun because Bob wanted to hunt as most boys did. He received a small 410-shotgun which he used for hunting partridge, a 12-gauge shotgun for hunting ducks, and a semi-automatic rifle. Bob's dad taught him how to use each of the guns and all of the safety requirements until George thought his son was able to go out on his own.

****

Between the sixth and eighth grades, Bob and his parents rode the DM&IR (Duluth, Minnesota and Iron Range) train between Leonidas and Eveleth and on to Virginia. It was clean and pleasant and they enjoyed the ride. When Bob turned sixteen, his father bought a car and Bob was able to drive it at times.

One day he drove some of his fellow Boy Scouts out to McKinley Park on Lake Vermilion where the Scouts were sponsoring a fishing contest. There was a limit of eight walleyes. Bob's dad had bought a rod and reel for him, but the reel wasn't working properly. It was so stiff and slow that if Bob got a bite, he just grabbed hold of the line and hand-over-hand hauled the fish in. He caught his limit that day, won an award, and brought the fish home to his mother.

****

George Givens was one of the fortunate employees at the Oliver Mining company who was permitted to rent a nice five-bedroom house for $7.50 a month. The mining company assumed all of the repairs on it and it was the home in which Bob grew up.

The Depression years were hard on nearly everyone. The Leonidas School had a school bank in which students were allowed to deposit a nickel, a dime, or whatever they could. Bob had earned a fair amount of money doing various chores over the years and had accumulated $42 in the school bank. Once during that time, the mine shut down. People in Leonidas and the surrounding area were hard-pressed to make ends meet, including George and Laura Givens. In spite of their meager rent, Bob's parents were forced to use the money their son had in his school bank account. Knowing that it broke their hearts to have to resort to that, Bob willingly gave it to them, and it was a moment of great pride—"A chance to pay them back for all they had done for me," Bob said.

2

Decisions, Decisions

B Y THE TIME HE REACHED THE 11TH GRADE, Bob had apparently spent too much time in the woods and not doing his homework. He wasn't doing well in school. He claimed, "I would'a got an 'A' in football, though." After the year was half over, Bob chose to quit school.

His dad was a WWI veteran and Bob admired him for that. Bob also had a friend whose older brother was in the Navy, serving on the USS *Maryland*. Bob had met the sailor earlier that year. He told Bob all about the Navy and how much he liked it.

Frustrated because he was doing poorly in school, Bob made a decision which he shared with no one. Instead of heading to school one day, he went to the Eveleth Post Office to see the Navy recruiter. After a brief interview, the recruiter gave him the entrance exams. Bob felt he had done a good job. The recruiter came back into the room with the test results. While the written part of the exam was fine, Bob was stunned into silence as the man told him something he had never imagined about himself: he was colorblind. Then came the chilling words, "I'm sorry, son. We don't want you."

Bob's world spun out of control as he grappled with the unbelievable news. This could not be happening! He had his heart set on joining the Navy. He somehow mustered the strength to rise from the chair. He trudged across the room and out the door. Dragging his feet all the way home, he was one dejected boy.

The look on her son's face when he came through the front door was like nothing Laura Givens had ever seen before.

"What's the matter?" she half-whispered. Bob explained that he had quit school and gone to see the Navy recruiter. He told her that he thought he did fine on the entrance exams. Then he relayed the shocking news that they didn't want him because he was colorblind.

Seeming to take it all in stride, Laura Givens replied, "Well, what are you going to do now? You're not going to lay around here."

"I don't know!" Bob shouted as he fought back the tears that threatened to burst forth. There was no doubt about it now. He knew he had to grow up and face the consequences of his actions.

The Civilian Conservation Corps, known as the CCC, was run by the U.S. Army and the U.S. Forest Service, and it employed many men in the area. Among the things the Corps was responsible for was planting trees, fighting fires, constructing shelters in the parks, and building dams in some of the lakes.

After serious thought and discussion with his family and friends, Bob chose to join the CCC. Some of his friends had joined and it was the only thing he could think of doing where he could be of some use. It turned out to be a positive experience for him. He learned many new things in the Corps, such as the military style of making a bed. There were inspections and mess halls, just like in the army. Bob got his first taste of military life in the CCC — and he liked it. He said, "It kept me out of trouble and made a man out of me."

Each member of the Civilian Conservation Corps was paid $30 a month. $7.50 was paid over the table for Bob's pocket. $7.50 went into savings for when he got out, and $15 went to his parents. Bob was assigned to Camp 3702 by Luna Lake at nearby Chisholm, Minnesota.

Most of the time his job consisted of planting Norway pines as part of the Superior National Forest.

The bad news was that you could only remain in the CCC for six months. They tried to give as many people as possible the opportunity to make some money. Reluctantly, when his half-year was over, Bob returned home for the rest of the summer.

In the fall of 1941, when the leaves bid farewell to the trees and began to swirl around the streets, school bells started ringing. With another surprise move, Bob announced, "I'm going back to school." He repeated the 11th grade and completed it.

In the summer of 1942 Bob had to get a job. He was hired by the DM&IR railroad as part of a track gang. Their job was to tamp down the railroad ties to keep the tracks level. They used a shovel to push crushed rock under the ties (a guy who did this work was known as a "Gandy Dancer.") Bob was paid $4.44 a day and worked there only a month before deciding to try to get a job at the Oliver Mine. His father had a good record there and they told Bob, "If you're as good as him, we'll give you a job." He worked in the mine for the next two months.

It was early September when as always, the school bells started ringing. Bob had thought long and hard about his education and now felt that he was finished with school. His persistent desire to be in the service had been burning inside him. One day as his mother had just finished washing the dishes, Bob strolled into the kitchen and addressed her with, "Come on, Mom – let's go to Duluth and talk to the military recruiters there." He was still hopeful that perhaps they could use him in some way.

When they got to the Armory, they saw that tables were set up along the perimeter of a large room. Recruiters from all branches of the service were there, and Bob was hoping for a miracle. The words of the Navy recruiter more than a year previously telling him that they didn't want him were as clear as the day Bob had first heard them.

As he walked along the row of tables, the recruiter from the Air Corps shouted, "We need one good man!"

Sullenly, Bob walked up to him and said, "I have always wanted to fly. I was in a club and for years I made model airplanes. I got to ride in a plane twice, but you don't want me because I'm colorblind."

The recruiter's eyes got big and he exclaimed, "Oh yes we do! A guy who's colorblind can spot camouflage on the ground way better than a guy with normal vision!"

In disbelief, Bob stiffened as both of his hands flew up in the air.

"Mister, you've got your man!" he shouted. With the greatest amount of surprise at this amazing turn of events, Bob and his mother were filled with joy. He signed on the dotted line and proudly announced, "I made it!"

3

Reporting for Duty

T HE EXACT STARTING DATE OF WORLD WAR II is uncertain. More than thirty countries were eventually involved and massive numbers of deaths resulted.

In 1937 Japan and China were engaged in war and Japan was determined to conquer Asia.

Then the Japanese turned their forces against the United States in a surprise attack at Pearl Harbor on December 7, 1941, resulting in the deaths of more than 2,000 Americans and nearly half as many others.

Meanwhile, countries in Europe were also at war, which had begun in 1939 when Germany invaded Poland. Adolph Hitler and his Nazi regime were determined to dominate as much of Europe as possible while exterminating all but pure-bred Germans, referred to as "Aryans." This, in turn, resulted in the infamous Holocaust in which more than six million Jewish people were systematically exterminated and nearly half that number of non-Jews perished from Nazi brutality.*

While there was real danger in military service during wartime, the Pearl Harbor attack had been unprovoked and retaliation was justified in the minds of most Americans. Also, word of Nazi atrocities and Hitler's domination of several European countries was spreading. Young men were volunteering and being drafted all over the United States.

Not having much formal education themselves, Bob's parents had never said much about his quitting school and they were proud of his decision to join the Air Corps, as it was called in those days. Bob was eighteen years old and admittedly, "full of piss and vinegar." Like many young people, he was fearless. He never had the fear of possibly being killed. It was the last thing on his mind at that time.

One thing he was concerned about though was fighting in Japan. He had heard that there were snakes everywhere over there, and Bob hated snakes. He knew that if he had a choice to go to Europe or Japan, he would definitely choose Europe. Bob was assigned a date to report to Fort Snelling in St. Paul, Minnesota.

Bob Givens was one proud and happy young man when he left home in Leonidas. While he was aware of the potential danger, he really did just want to serve his country — and to be able to do it while flying — well, that was the icing on the

---

*Wikipedia: "World War II," accessed September 28,2016 (https://en.wikipedia.org); "Holocaust," accessed September 28, 2016 (https://en.wikipedia.org); "Aryan Race," accessed September 28, 2016 (https:/en.wikipedia.org).

cake. He was convinced that the United States was the best country in the world. Bob said, "I'd be damned if I'd be drafted." He believed that the most honorable thing to do was to volunteer, and he had heard that if you volunteered you would get what you wanted.

In the fall of 1942 Bob traveled to Fort Snelling. Stretched along the high banks of the Mississippi River, the fort was abuzz with processing procedures for new recruits. Some of the young men fidgeted nervously, while others like Bob were excited and composed. Bob had to relate his personal history and go through a lot of "red tape" that first day.

The new airmen were outfitted with uniforms, which Bob found thrilling. At that time, both the Air Corps and the Army were stationed at Fort Snelling and they had the same tan uniforms. (In 1949 the Air Corps became known as the Air Force and they changed the color of their uniforms to blue.)

4

Basic on the Beach

T HE FOLLOWING DAY, ROBERT GIVENS was on a train headed for a hot spot, although not at all where he would have expected to be sent during a time of war. That train headed south then east and then southeast—all the way down to Miami Beach! It is a fact that during that time Uncle Sam had taken over the entire beach—hotels, restaurants, shops, and all.

The elevators in the hotels had been disabled. This was, after all, Basic Training. These young men were destined to get plenty of exercise, beginning with walking up and down the stairs. Soon they started marching and doing drills on the sand of that famous beachfront.

One warm and sunny day, Bob and a group of recruits were marched out to the beach in front of a large hotel for a maneuver. They were instructed to wade out into chest-deep water. Once there, they were to remove their pants and tie

Bob in the water at Miami Beach.

the legs together in a knot. Next, they were told to hold the pants over their head and whip them down quickly so that they would fill with air like a balloon. It was to be used as an emergency life preserver, and it would hold you up for a while if you did it right.

Basic training lasted about thirty days and involved mainly marching and drills, but it was where they also learned commands. When the group was asked if anyone wanted to volunteer to act as temporary Drill Sergeant, Bob held up his hand. He shouted out commands and the group responded appropriately, much to his delight.

One day when the rain set in and the wind blasted the coast, high waves pounded the beach relentlessly. It was an experience most of the young men were unaccustomed to, since the majority of them had not been raised in coastal ocean areas. Like a cymbal player repeating the same stanza over and over again, the crashing blows against the sand came like clockwork. It got to be nerve-wracking after a while, but the weather wasn't the only thing making Bob nervous that day.

His entire unit was ordered to report to a room in a nearby hotel for vision testing. Dreading that he may be dismissed after this long, Bob could hardly breathe as he waited his turn to enter the testing room. When his last name was called, Bob went into the room where there was a man with nothing more than a box of yarn. The yarn had been cut into equal lengths and there were several of each various color. Bob froze at the thought. Then the man in charge told him to get all of the green strands. Bob's hands went to work, ferreting out a good number of the strands.

Luck was on his side because he passed the test, proving something significant: he was not totally colorblind, as he had previously thought. It was a happy day for young Robert Givens and definitely something to write home about. Bob was really enjoying his induction into the military, but he did miss his parents and being home. He became a faithful letter-writer throughout his years in the service, always wanting to keep the folks back home informed of his daily experiences.

Just as his Basic Training was coming to an end, a group of 400-500 guys gathered to listen to a man who was looking for volunteers to go to aerial gunnery school. He explained that it would involve six weeks of training, and upon graduation, you would be classified as a "buck sergeant." You would have three stripes and silver wings on your uniform! Bob's eyes were bulging! What was not to like?

Then the recruiter added, "The average life expectancy of an aerial gunner in combat is two minutes. How many volunteers do I have?" Five or six guys put their hands up, and that is how Robert Gordon Givens got into Aerial Gunnery School. He shouted aloud, "Now I know I'm gonna fly!"

5

A Tale of Two Schools

I T WASN'T LONG AFTER BOB HAD VOLUNTEERED for Aerial Gunnery School that he was on a train headed for Harlingen, Texas, close to the Mexican border. Shortly after his arrival, he was faced with a frightful dilemma. Yet another vision test was required and the prospect of it had his stomach in knots. He really wanted to be a gunner. The new recruits stood in line to take the test. Seated at the front of the room was a man with a book Bob recognized. The contents of that book had devastated him once before with the Navy recruiter in Eveleth. It was full of large dots in many different colors. This time it was important not to be colorblind, and Bob was in trouble.

Praying for a miracle, he had beads of sweat crowning his forehead. Behind him was a fellow who had chatted with him earlier. In desperation, Bob quietly spoke to him, begging him to please whisper the answers. When the guys ahead of him had moved out, Bob was finally at the front of the line. As the dots were displayed, barely-audible answers flowed into Bob's ears, and gratefully, he passed the test.

Bob's hunting experience in prior years was helpful now that shooting was the primary focus of gunnery school. He had handled a variety of guns over the years and had shot plenty of birds and game in the woods by his home. During the first week at this school, recruits spent much of the time in a room that resembled an arcade with guns. They were taught to lead with their guns, that is to shoot ahead of a moving target.

Aircraft I.D. was another topic of study. A picture of a plane such as a Messerschmitt would be presented and described. The recruits were required to learn all about each aircraft they may encounter and to instantly recognize its type. The German planes (Luftwaffe, as they were called,) always had the black "Iron Cross" on their sides, while the U.S. planes were readily identified by a white star on both sides of the fuselage.

Several weeks were devoted to the skills of bore sighting. They were taught to remove the bore from the gun and make sure it was on target. Then they were required to take apart a 50-caliber machine gun and spread all of the parts on the floor. It didn't end there, of course. Each man was then ordered to re-assemble all of the parts. In the end, they had to do the entire process blindfolded.

The gunsites were like motorcycle grips. Range dimension was on the right-hand grip (known as Sight Reticles.) They were used to line up the Range Dimension Dial — 0-40 feet, depending on the wing span of the targeted aircraft.

Bob wearing his vest and parachute
harness at Harlingen, Texas.

Mastering the use of the Sight Reticles was an integral part
of the top turret gunner's responsibility.

Bob had enjoyed the challenges of this training, but the
last week was the most fun. Two planes went up at a time,
one with a sleeve target attached behind it. The ammo was
colored differently for each gunner, and it would leave a ring
of color on the target if you hit it. The recruits each had an
opportunity to take his turn shooting at the target. A passing

score was six hits on the moving target. Bob Givens scored twelve on his first attempt.

Another type of target practice they experienced was shooting at objects in the water. After taking off in a B-34, each prospective gunner was instructed to lie down on the floor of the plane where there was an opening. Targets had been placed in the water below and the colored ammo was used again. Shooting with a lead was stressed in their previous instruction regarding moving targets, and the importance of shooting in that manner at objects in the water was once again apparent.

Upon completion of Aerial Gunnery School, those who qualified were sent to a room for official photos. A large belt heavily laden with ammo was draped over each individual's shoulder and a picture was taken. Bob was bursting with pride and truly felt like he had become a man, even though he was only eighteen years old. That picture was sent home just as soon as possible.

A "flight engineer" and a "top gunner" were Bob's new designations. He was instructed on the method of transferring fuel from the wingtip tanks to a center tank. This was necessary since the wings were often hit during combat, and it reduced the danger of an explosion.

Bob was feeling "damn good," and wondering where he would be sent next. He and his fellow recruits were split up after that and Bob never saw any of them again.

Somewhere along the line in a great deal of testing, Bob must have been given one that involved gears. He was ordered to another school in Texas. This time it was Airplane Mechanics School in Amarillo. He was about to

Bob fresh out of Gunnery School, 1943.

learn every part of an airplane engine—in other words—
what makes it tick.

Bob was surprised to see that one of the instructors there
was a guy from Eveleth, Minnesota, near his home. This was
an intensive, complicated training with the emphasis on every
working part of the aircraft. Bob was taught that it was his
responsibility to direct the pilot to perform functions such as

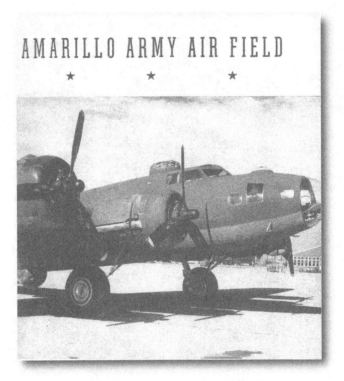

A B-17 at Amarillo Army Air Field, Amarillo, Texas.

"feather the engine," or "pull up the cowl flaps" in order to keep the engine cooler. It took four months to complete this school.

There was a song that went, "The Sands of Amarillo are a-stickin' on my pillow." Bob would tell you that is true. The wind blew sand everywhere and the young man from northern Minnesota had never been so cold in his life. The barracks had to be cabled down due to the powerful winds.

There was also a hailstorm. Hail larger than golf balls hammered the area breaking every exposed bulb as well as puncturing the canvas that covered the fuselages of several planes.

Soon after completing Aircraft Maintenance School, Bob was shipped by train to Salt Lake City, Utah, for crew assignment. He was excited — "rarin' to go!" He had a goal: to be actually on a B-17 and flying his missions. That goal was getting ever closer as the train headed northwest.

6

Final Training

ONCE AT THE BASE AT SALT LAKE, the men got settled in their temporary quarters, since this was just a stopover on their way further north. They were told to report to a huge building where there were both officers and enlisted men. Every man was handed a number. Bob Givens got #1. Then they were told to go around the room and seek out all of the others with a number the same as theirs. There were ten total in Bob's group, including six enlisted and four officers. This was his crew. The first guy who had answered, "I have #1," was their tail gunner. It was a fun and novel way to meet your crewmates.

They were only in Salt Lake overnight, then on another train headed for Moses Lake, Washington for the first of three, sixty-hour final phases of training. Moses Lake was one of the few places in the country at that time with 10,000-foot runways.

While there, it was critical to determine who could or could not withstand and function at high altitudes. Several guys were placed in a pressure chamber that simulated flying at 40,000-50,000 feet. As the pressure increased, there was a visible difference in the men. While some were trying to fight it, they were nonetheless turning blue and they clearly couldn't take it. Robert Givens lasted the whole way and he felt great. As a result, he was assigned to heavy four-engine bombers. Some of the others were assigned medium-to-light bombers.

During the first phase of this training, they had sixty hours of flight. There were many "round robins," where they would take off, circle the field, land, and repeat the process again and again. The purpose of this training was to help familiarize every man with the plane throughout a flight and to acquaint him with his position. Each man needed to realize that he was part of a crew and it was essential that they all work together. Equally important was the job that each individual was assigned to perform. They would take turns going around the plane in order with each guy calling out the position of an imaginary plane circling theirs. It might go from "Twelve o'clock on" and from high to low ("Three o'clock low," for example) to indicate the position of another plane so that they could adjust the position of their guns.

Bob was shipped to Ephrata, Washington for Phase 2 of the final training. An additional sixty hours were required for the bombadiers to practice dropping bombs. Much time was spent with practice bombs, which contained colored powder that would leave a mark where they landed. Bob was designated the engineer/top turret gunner. In addition to advanced gunnery training, he was instructed in how to read instruments and to complete "Form 1" for each flight. This involved listing each member of the crew and the condition of the plane. A full crew had one bombardier, a navigator, pilot, co-pilot, a radio operator, two waist gunners, a tail gunner, a ball-turret gunner, and an engineer/top gunner.

Still not finished with his training, Bob boarded a train for Phase 3. This time he was headed back to Sioux City, Iowa and he was looking forward to winding up his training. These final sixty hours focused on night flight training and once more involved practice bombs. The purpose of these flights was again primarily for the bombardier.

In a final address to the men, the instructor told them that each one was now prepared to do his job. He said it was indeed an honor to wear that uniform and they should be very proud of serving their country in the fight for freedom. No one was more proud than Bob Givens.

His training finally complete, Bob was on yet another train, this time headed for Grand Island, Nebraska. The Air Corps troops would be leaving from there to go overseas. When he learned that they were getting a brand-new B-17G, all silver and shiny, Bob was nothing short of elated! He was thrilled to explore every part of the plane, especially the section where the top turret was located. This was his space and he loved it. Before heading overseas, Bob and several of his comrades went on leave together and partied in anticipation of the experiences to come.

As excited as Bob was with that new B-17G, he was equally looking forward to the arrival of his mom and dad.

Bob in a jeep at the Grand Island, Nebraska Air Base.

They were taking their first long-distance train trip to visit their son before he went off to war. Bob was anxiously awaiting their arrival for days. It was a very happy day when the train pulled into the Grand Island station as his parents stepped off and were joyously reunited with the young man now known as Staff Sergeant Robert Givens.

They were taken by a cab to the base, where Bob happily showed them around. George and Laura Givens were also given a tour of the plane that would fly their son to Europe. While it was shiny and solid-looking, George Givens pushed his hand against the side of the aircraft and said, "Son, this isn't very strong!"

With a chuckle, Bob replied, "It's an airplane, Dad, not a tank!" His parents got to meet the entire crew and they were very proud of their son. They naturally had concerns for his safety, but they did not voice them to Bob. They knew how hard he had worked to get where he was and that the time had come to let him go.

When the crew was ordered to start calibrating the instruments aboard the plane, all guests had to depart. It had been a brief visit, but they were all grateful for the opportunity to see each other again. Staff Sergeant Givens gave his mom and dad a kiss and a hug and they said their good-by's. With heavy hearts and a good deal of pride, his parents returned to a nearby hotel. They would take the train back home the next day.

Each plane accommodated a ten-man crew and Bob got along with all of them, although he was closest to the pilot and the bombardier. While in the air, they all called each other by their first names. Once on the ground, however, officers were treated with respect and addressed properly.

The crew became a band of brothers, a closely-knit group who realized that each of them was responsible for the safety of all. If one man had a dollar, ten cents belonged to each man. Bob's group never had any friction between the men, but others occasionally did. As part of the phase training, a lead pilot was assigned to the group to determine whether or not they got along. If not, one or two were removed and it got settled. The pilot was the "top dog." If two guys were not getting along, it had to be reported to the pilot, who would attempt to settle the problem himself. If they could

The new B-17G that would fly Bob and his crew overseas.

not leave and shake hands, they were called on the carpet with the senior officers.

The pilot was respected by the crew, and to some like Bob, the pilot was revered. Their lives were in his hands, although he once stated, "If you guys don't shoot straight, it's my ass too!"

7

Hopping Across the Big Pond

B OB AND HIS CREWMATES ROSE EARLY the next morning. They showered, got dressed, ate breakfast, then headed out to the plane. There it sat, like a big silver bird. Excitement ran high as the guys climbed up and piled inside, each drawn to his designated spot like a magnet. They ran all of the preliminary protocols and checks on the equipment. Before long, they were taxiing down the runway. Their plane got in line with several others, and one-by-one, they took off. When it was their turn, the props on Bob's plane revved up loudly and the pilot shouted, "Here we go, boys!" They sped down the runway, then lifted off.

They were headed east, to Bangor, Maine, but the weather there was bad and they were diverted to Manchester, New Hampshire instead. They were taking the "northern route to Europe" and their trip was a bit like playing hopscotch. They spent the first night in Manchester, then took off the next morning for Goose Bay, Labrador, where they spent the second night. The following morning, they flew to Meek Field, Iceland, where they spent the third night. The next morning, they left for Preswick, Scotland.

They had a serious problem when they approached Preswick. The airfield was well-camouflaged, in fact, more so than usual. The pilot and co-pilot were unable to spot the runway and they were circling the area in search of it. The crew was aware of the situation and were growing concerned when Bob shouted, "There it is!" He was the only one who could see it. Bob was feeling pretty good about that. Once he pointed it out, the others were able to spot it. Everything had been painted to blend in with the surroundings. The color-blindness he had once feared was now a valuable asset.

For as much as they had looked forward to their arrival in Preswick, they were soon all disappointed. They were so proud of their new B17G and felt bonded with it after their arduous trip across the ocean. Almost immediately after their arrival, they were ordered to turn it over for "modifications." Bob and his crew were nothing short of "broken-hearted."

8

Home Sweet Home Base

A FTER ONE NIGHT AT PRESWICK, BOB and his crew were boarding a train for the U.S. bomber base in England. Their home base was in a small town called Attleborough. Upon their arrival, they were escorted to the barracks, (which were Quonset huts,) by a sergeant who turned to Bob inside and said, "This is your bunk."

The bed had another man's name on it, and Bob asked, "What about that guy?"

With a visibly stiffened upper lip, the sergeant replied, "He won't be back. He got shot down."

In the days following, they had to practice flights and a lot of formation flying. During the war, England's Royal Air Force (RAF) flew one behind another. The U.S., on the other hand, would have 800-900 planes flying closely together in one enormous formation.

Quonset huts at Home Base in England.

The quaint town of Attleborough, England.

There was an armament shop at the Home Base where the gunners worked on 50-calibre machine guns. For each man, the shop had a gun that had his name on it. Bob was responsible for cleaning the two top turret guns.

Flying in formation, heading for designated targets.

At 50,000-60,000 feet, the temperature can be fifty below zero. The high altitude bomber crews had to wear protective gear to survive. The first inflatable life preserver was nicknamed the "Mae West" after the buxom actress popular in Vaudeville and on Broadway during World War II. The crew was outfitted in electric flying suits (similar to wet diving suits.) These suits were plugged into the plane's electrical system for warmth. Next came a big jacket and pants, both made of sheepskin, which went over the electric suit. Then came the Mae West life vest, and last was the parachute and harness. No wonder when the crew would walk toward the plane in their full gear, others would say, "Here come the men from Mars!"

While in Attleborough, England, Bob and his crew visited a small pub which was actually just a little "hole-in-the-wall." Staff Sergeant Givens was feeling particularly emboldened when they first strolled in. He looked around and in a loud voice asked, "Isn't there any nicer place to go have a beer around here?"

Among chuckles of laughter from the locals, one of them loudly retorted, "Geez, Buddy, this is it! You're not in the States, you know. You're in jolly old England!"

Mission One

A FTER A COUPLE OF WEEKS AT HOME BASE, Bob and his crew were set to go on their first mission. This is what they had been working for and they were all eager to get going. For Bob, this was even more exciting than that first flight in a J3 Cub with the pilot from Virginia, Minnesota years before. This time, he was trained and qualified to make a difference on a very important mission in a very big war.

Adolph Hitler had been in the headlines for several years. Well before Bob Givens had enlisted, he had followed the war in newspapers, the radio, school, and conversations with family and friends. The more Bob learned about Hitler, the more he felt hatred toward the brutal, power-hungry dictator.

There were two movie theaters (the State and the Regent) in Eveleth, Minnesota when Bob was growing up. A newsreel was always run before the main feature and it brought world events to the silver screen in theaters across America. There was footage of the British Prime Minister Neville Chamberlain traveling to Germany in an attempt to talk peace with Hitler, which soon proved to be futile. The newsreels depicted Adolph Hitler gaining so much power he was trying to take over the world like Napoleon. They were also increasingly reporting the fact that he was mesmerizing the masses with his forceful rhetoric.

So it was that Bob Givens was in sync with his crewmates in their dedication to a whole-hearted belief in the righteousness of their participation in this war. Their first mission was to a German-occupied base in Chatoduon, France. As their plane took off that morning, every man was in position and ready to go. A mission was very serious business. You didn't dare talk on the intercom once it began. Anticipation ran high as the plane climbed into the clouds.

Bob was in the highest spot on the B-17. He was the top turret gunner and he operated two fully-loaded 50-caliber machine guns which were mounted on a swivel base. His position was capped by a Plexiglass half-bubble mounted onto the top of the fuselage. He had a 360-degree view of the space surrounding the plane. Most of their designated targets that day were so-called "marshalling yards" (a.k.a. railroad yards,) and ball-bearing plants.

There was, however, a horrifying incident they were witness to on that mission. Two of the B-17's in Bob's squadron were immediately in front of his plane when they received direct hits from "flak" guns. Right before their eyes, Bob and his crew watched in dismay as two or three guys bailed out with their parachutes just prior to the blinding explosions of their planes.

Bob had an eagle-eye's view of the shocking scene and the reality of where he was slapped him across the face in that moment. He seriously thought, *Count your blessings, Robert Gordon Givens!* On each mission after that, he was "a-prayin."

Their first mission was completed and they returned to Home Base with a good amount of pride. Bob Givens had truly become a "Top Gun."

10

The First Five

I T IS A SAD FACT THAT DURING THE FIRST Berlin raid, of which Bob was not a part, a total of sixty B-17s were lost in one day. Each plane had a crew of ten. The loss of those planes was enormous, but the loss of hundreds of men was devastating.

Before and after every mission, there were mandatory briefings. The entire crew was summoned to a room where they sat around a table. Briefings prior to a mission were to discuss the nature of the forthcoming mission and to pinpoint locations and desired outcomes. Post briefings were different. After a mission, they were supposed to divulge what they had observed while in the air. The commander would say, "Well, boys, what did you see today? See anything interesting?"

The officers needed to learn everything they could to help with further missions. To that end, there was "liquid encouragement" in the form of "a big ol' jug of booze" on the table, which was available to all of the guys, and it "made you shoot your mouth off." The men were usually smart enough though not to abuse the liquor because 4:00 a.m. came mighty early the next morning and they didn't want to suffer from a hangover.

There is an old expression that goes: "What is all that flak?" Flak during World War II consisted of pieces of metal from explosives that were shot high into the air by canons on the ground. Canons were strategically spaced from the coast around targeted areas. Surrounding the towns were JU88s (big anti-aircraft guns.) Sometimes the Germans would have a B-17 that had crash-landed and they would repair it to fly again. Flying incognito, it was used to report the speed and position of the Allied planes so they could set the JU88s accordingly.

Flak was the cause of many planes going down. Some of the U.S. planes, such as Bob's, had a radio operator who had a parachute with boxes and bags of cellophane attached to it. When released, these items appeared on the Germans' radar and it distracted them. As an evasive tactic, it often worked.

On one of Bob's missions, the flak was exceptionally heavy. While they were dodging the worst of it, a formidable adversary appeared on the horizon. What may well have been the best of all World War II fighter planes, the Messerschmitt B-109 housed the largest engine on the smallest body. The ominous Iron Cross was emblazoned on its sides, and it literally zoomed toward them. Bob had to swing his guns around to get a shot at it, and he did, but it was too late. With regret, he watched that one get away. On missions such as that, things happened so fast, you didn't have time to think about them for long. You just had to get over it. Several more missions followed and Bob had plenty of action.

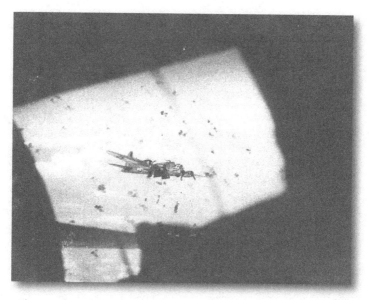

Photo taken from inside a B-17 during a bombing run as the planes try to dodge enemy flak.

As Bob and his crew were returning to England following another raid, they were looking for the white cliffs of Dover, which they perceived as the gate to their Home Base. Their first five missions had been successful and they had reason to celebrate.

A plane's bomb load depended upon the nature of each mission. Some required just one 5000-pound bomb, while others would use ten 500-pound bombs or some incendiaries

A B-17 named "Flak Shy Lady."

if fire on the ground was called for. Bob and his crew dropped many bombs during their first five missions. They had often encountered flak and were fired upon as they dropped their bombs and returned fire. Nevertheless, they were able each time to get back to Home Base with holes, gashes, and scrapes to be repaired on the plane before their next assignment.

After five successful missions over enemy territory, each crew member was awarded the Air Medal. If he got five more, he was awarded an oak-leaf cluster, then another cluster for additional five missions up to twenty-five. The Distinguished Flying Cross was awarded to those few individuals who survived twenty-five successful missions over enemy territory. It is a cherished and highly-respected honor. Bob had already earned the Air Medal. He was, of course, proud.

A B-17 delivering its load.

The pilot of the plane was supposed to censor the mail of each of his crew. The men were not allowed to describe or make any reference or comments about their missions. When Bob called home, he would tell his dad to "scratch another one off." It was their version of a secret code for "another successful mission."

People in the neighboring villages around the Home Base respected the U.S. military. One English woman lived in a small house near the perimeter of the base and she would wash clothes for Bob and his crewmates. She called them "son," just like her own children. They paid her generously. Clean clothes gained priority when the crew was granted a leave to go to London.

The military provided fully-paid leaves of absence for the

men when they were due. Bob had five missions under his belt with twenty more to go, then he could go home to his mom and dad. He had some Flak Leave and the military arranged for several of the guys to go on a tour of London and the surrounding area. They visited the London Bridge, Big Ben, Westminster Abbey, Piccadilly Circus, and even Stratford-Upon-Avon (home of William Shakespeare.)

While on this tour, they naturally went into pubs. Sometimes the G.I.s would get in line and drink a pub dry. The pub maid would say, "What'll ya 'ave?"

"Whata ya got?" they'd ask.

"Mild, bitter, and off and off," she'd yell, describing the types of beer or ale they served.

Once, when Bob was in a cocky mood, he shouted, "I own this here British Isles!"

With narrowed eyes, the pub maid turned and glared at him, demanding, "Whata ya mean?"

"I own you!" the twenty-year-old said grinning at her.

She blasted him with, "Ya bloody Yanks! You're over here, over-paid, and over-sexed!"

That brought cheers from the crowd.

While in another pub one day, Bob met a couple of guys who already had twenty-five missions. They had gone home on leave and then returned for a second tour. Later he heard that both of them had gone down.

11

Out of the Blue

I T WAS APRIL 11, 1944 — THE NIGHT BEFORE Bob's sixth mission. They had just returned from Flak Leave. Two crews were housed in each Quonset hut. Bob's crew was happy to get back, but a bit disgusted because while they were on leave, some of the other guys got additional missions ahead of them. Now they were anxious to catch up and Bob was "rarin' to go."

By 4:00 a.m. the following morning, they were up, getting into full gear except for their chutes. The rumble of a truck engine grew closer as Bob and his crewmates headed out into the cold, penetrating darkness to wait for their ride to the mess hall. Once there, they got in line for breakfast and each man picked up a tray. The cook would yell, "How d'ya want your eggs?" They were real eggs, not the powdered ones. The Air Corps took care of their men.

After breakfast, they reported to another building for a briefing. On the wall was a big map, covered with a cloth-like a sheet. When everyone was seated, the commanding officer pulled a string and the cloth fell off — revealing the location in Germany of their upcoming mission — and some of the details were announced.

Upon conclusion of the briefing, some of the crew walked to the armament shop. There they would get machine guns and chest pack chutes. That type of parachute was strapped into a harness which was worn around the torso. The guns and the chutes were labeled with each man's name.

Soon they were back in the "6x6," which was a tandem truck with a canvas top and benches along the sides in back. These trucks could transport ten to twelve guys. That morning, the 6x6 rolled up to the planes, which were fueled up, loaded, and ready to go.

The men got out of the truck, leaving their guns and chutes, and walked toward their B-17. All six enlisted men lined up in front of the plane. One-at-a-time, they would push each of the four propellers, which would force the oil to push back into the engine so it would be ready for take-off. After completing that task, they went back to the truck to retrieve their guns and parachutes. Then they returned to the plane, climbed onboard, and put their guns in place.

The ammunition was already on the plane, having been loaded there by the Master Sergeant, who was the crew chief on the ground. He handed Bob Givens the "Form 1," on which Bob was required to list the name, rank, and serial number of each guy on board. Also, if there was anything out of working order on the plane that was observed during the flight, it had to be noted. Each man had chores he needed to do on the plane before takeoff.

The officers had a separate briefing after the initial one earlier. Their second briefing outlined the specifics of the upcoming mission and the formation they would be flying. There were hundreds of planes involved in this mission and careful coordination was essential. Following this briefing, the officers boarded the plane with everyone else already in position. The pilot got out a checklist and carefully went over everything outlined on it. Then they began to start up the aircraft.

After they got the engines running, Bob's plane headed out into the darkness toward the end of the runway. There was a guy standing at the end of the runway with a light. Two lines of planes faced him. When he flashed the light, the plane to the right took off. The pilot had to be careful not to get caught in the "prop wash" from the previous plane's takeoff. Thirty seconds later, he flashed the light again, and Bob's plane headed down the runway, accelerating to top speed, then lifting off.

The plane climbed rapidly to get into the formation. It took anywhere from sixty to ninety minutes to achieve full formation at 24,000 feet, since there were around eight hundred planes total!

There were three main divisions within the formation and each one had its own target. They wanted to keep the *Luftwaffe* split up, chasing the Allied planes in different directions. That way, the Germans would become confused and they could not deal with 800 planes against them in the air. The bomb squadrons, like Bob's, flew in a tight formation with a first echelon of three planes including the lead plane, a second echelon of three more, and a final plane referred to as "Tail End Charlie." It was well-planned. However, it is amazing there were not more accidents, given the proximity of so many aircraft flying together!

Each bomb group consisted of four bomb squadrons. Each squadron put up seven planes in a mission. The fourth squadron would fly along for a period of time to act as subs in case any of the planes had trouble. Then they would return to the base and take the day off. Squadrons would rotate, taking turns at this assignment.

Everything went smoothly that morning as they got into one enormous formation at 24,000 feet and headed out over the North Sea. The pilot of Bob's plane gave the order to test-fire the guns and that went fine. Everything was "A-ok."

Bob was excited and proud to be part of a mission of this magnitude, flying close to their comrades in nearby planes. It was a clear day as the sky revealed a whisper of the morning light. They were sailing smoothly aloft. The plan was to head north toward the Arctic Circle, then do a "180," and head straight south into Germany. They knew the Germans would not be expecting an attack from the north.

Then suddenly, something went terribly wrong.

12

The Desperate Descent

B OB GIVENS WAS IN THE TOP TURRET OF A B-17, enjoying the best view in the house. They were surrounded 360 degrees by other planes flying in this giant formation far above the North Sea. Suddenly, with no warning, the left wing of his plane lifted sharply upward, jolting everyone on board out of position. As fast as it had gone up, it came down with great force and continued to swing, this time as the right wing lifted high in the air. It was chaos and everyone was stunned as the reality of the inevitable struck them. Bob's immediate thought, no doubt like most of the others, was, *I've gotta get out of here!*

His position in the top turret afforded no seat. Bob was standing, with his harness on, but his parachute was on the floor. It was attached to only one hook on his harness because a gunner could not operate with a bulky chest pack chute in front of him. He needed total freedom to swivel in his shooting position.

B-17 in flight. Note the top turret, which is like the one Bob flew in during his missions.

The right wing slammed down. Swinging to the left once more, this time it quickly jerked back and forth before it went full circle. The plane was clearly stalling and Bob needed to get out of it. His immediate plan was to go down to the bombardier's escape hatch and jump out from there. He was able to pick up his chute pack from the floor just before the plane started spiraling down.

Centrifugal force pinned Bob to the base of the turret. Large chunks of the plane were tearing off and he couldn't even unhook the oxygen. Hanging his head down, he choked, "*I guess I've had it!*" With a lack of oxygen, he fell into a state of unconsciousness.

The co-pilot had baled out the side window of the cockpit and watched as the top turret ripped right off the plane at over 20,000 feet. Bob Givens was in the top turret. With nothing to hold him in any longer, when the plane rolled upside down — he fell out.

With a fresh supply of oxygen, Bob shortly regained his senses only to face the shock of where he was — hurtling through space toward the icy waters of the North Sea far below! His first thought was, *Hey, I'm still alive!* Then he grabbed for his chute, but it wasn't there.

Bob frantically looked for his parachute. It wasn't above his head where it should have been! Then he saw it — off to one side tethered to a long strap. Bob started pulling it toward him, hand-over-hand, just as he had reeled in those eight fish in the Boy Scout fishing contest years earlier.

Against all odds, Bob got the chute, and with some difficulty, as one may only imagine, he snapped it onto the harness. He was mindful of his instructor's answer to the question, "What if the parachute doesn't open?"

"Well, son, you won't get another chance," had been the reply.

When Bob pulled the ripcord, he was not in a vertical position. As the chute burst open, it was a "hellava jolt," but Bob said out loud, "Thank God!" He looked down and saw the waters of the deep blue sea below — and his boots falling down ahead of him. Also, there were pieces of the plane floating in the water, but he saw no men. Bob was surely counting his blessings, while at the same time feeling real sorry for the ones who didn't make it.

Bob felt like he was hardly moving once the parachute opened. It was as if he were hanging on a big sky hook.

After a while, to his utmost relief, Bob saw an RAF plane approaching. It circled him twice. The second time, the pilot gave Bob a "thumbs-up." Bob returned the gesture, indicating that he was ok. The pilot dipped his wing and flew away.

13

Splashdown!

I T WAS TIME FOR BOB TO START THINKING of a plan for when he hit the water. He decided to open only one half of his Mae West vest, thinking he could more easily slip out of the chute harness that way. (One instructor he had in training told them to inflate both sides of the vest, then slip out of the harness so the chute wouldn't come down and smother you.) However, Bob thought it would make it more difficult to quickly get out of the harness and figured that the guy never had to use one himself. Bob was only a few feet above the waves when he took a deep breath and braced himself for the impact.

Hitting the water feet first, he entered the North Sea with no big splash. He was vertical by then and it was, according to Bob, "pretty slick." He had his wits about him, and he was dealing with each stage of this harrowing experience one step at a time.

Now he was far below the surface and he had his work cut out for him. With only half of his Mae West inflated and with all of the gear he was wearing, he had to really struggle upward. His arms pulled with all his might and his legs kicked like an outboard motor. The instant he finally breached the surface, Bob Givens heartily gasped as he inhaled the biggest breath of air in his life!

Then he noticed that he had not surfaced underneath the open parachute, which was lucky for him. There was enough wind that it had blown off to the side as he entered the water. He did not have to wrestle his way out from under it and there was no fear of suffocating because of it. Next, he looked around. No one was there. He was alone in the middle of the cold and choppy North Sea. However, he did not feel cold because of the warm gear he was wearing.

Oddly enough, he wasn't afraid. That was when his old Boy Scout training came in real handy. Bob did not panic in the water. He knew how to swim and float, and he tried to keep his focus on getting home.

When faced with one's own mortality, in a moment of desperation we sometimes make promises in an attempt to cheat death. Bob could only think about getting back to his parents.

As he inflated the other side of his Mae West vest, he pleaded out loud, "Dear Lord, please help me! I promise I'll go to church every day. I'll quit smoking and I'll quit drinking. Just get me back to my mom and dad!" There was no "tough boy" any more.

It was before noon. Bob had been told that a person would never survive for more than forty-five minutes in the North Sea at that time of year, regardless of the protective clothing he may be wearing. He was keenly aware that his time was limited and he felt like one of his old fishing bobbers as he bounced around on top of the freezing cold water. He had never felt more alone in his life. Treading water, Bob contemplated the depths below and continued to pray.

Thirty minutes later those prayers were answered when Bob heard the loud rumble of an aircraft engine. Out of the sky, lumbered the most beautiful thing he had ever seen. It was a big amphibious Walrus (RAF Air/Sea Rescue plane, capable of landing on the water!) The RAF pilot that had circled Bob earlier must have notified his base that a plane had gone down. The Walrus pilot brought that thing down to the water's surface like a giant kite. It was a sight to see as it skimmed across the water, creating a huge rooster tail behind it. The trouble was, it stopped a long way from Bob.

14

A Small Speck on a Big Sea

T HE SEA WAS ROUGH ENOUGH THAT Bob could never have seen three other men afloat some distance away. Still treading water, Bob waited hopefully now as the others were picked up. Several minutes later, the door on the big Walrus was closed and the engines revved up with a loud roar. Bob panicked then as he thought, *Oh, my God! They don't know I'm here!* He started to blow on the whistle attached to his Mae West. Naturally, they could hear nothing over the rumble of their engines. Bob was waving his arms frantically now, praying that they would see him.

He was just a speck on the surface of a large body of rough water, and he was a good distance away from them. How would they ever spot him? As he watched the huge aircraft maneuver across the water, it turned and started to come directly toward him. They did know he was there! They dropped two inflatable dinghies hooked together with a cable upwind of Bob. The idea was for him to grab the rope and get into one of the dinghies. Bob tried to swim toward them, but they were too far away and the sea was plenty rough. The dinghies kept drifting away from him.

The huge aircraft motored closer. A side door opened and two men stood in the doorway. They held out a pole with a hook on one end. He grabbed hold of it, and they were able to pull in a grateful Bob Givens.

Once aboard the Walrus, he was laid on the floor alongside the three others and covered with blankets. They checked his hands and saw that they were blue. Bob had been in the water for almost an hour.

The aircraft took off "like nobody's business" and the crew aboard was busy trying to keep the rescued men warm. They were bundled tightly from head to foot. It was just a short flight back to England. They approached land and were soon on the runway when there was a loud blast. The big plane started to bounce roughly. A tire had blown and they spun around once or twice before coming to a stop. Even though this was another unnerving episode, Bob Givens was one happy man—thankful to the good Lord to be back on solid ground.

15

New Quarters

T HEY WERE FIRST TAKEN TO A SMALL CLINIC where they were checked out and evaluated to determine whether they should go back to the base or to the hospital. Bob's adrenaline must have been pumping in high gear because he felt no pain. He was lying on a gurney when he decided he wanted to see who else had survived from his crew. They hadn't been able to see each other on the Walrus because they were so bundled up and they were taken off the plane one-at-a-time. As Bob tried to raise his head to look at the others, he found that he couldn't do it. He yelled, "Hey! Something's wrong over here!"

Bob was rolled over onto his stomach and the doctor tapped his back with his fingers, then announced, "You're going to the hospital." They rolled him over again. When he was hurled around in the turret, he apparently got a gash on his head that he was unaware of. Before he knew what was happening, the doctor started stitching it up and Bob yelled, "Hey, Doc, what are you doin'?"

The doctor nonchalantly replied, "Oh, you've got a little scratch here." Bob got nearly twelve stitches on his head.

The three other crewmen who survived were the co-pilot and the two waist gunners. They were transported back to the Home Base while Bob was loaded into a small ambulance. He was mourning the loss of the rest of his crew. "Six wonderful guys died that day," he whispered. He was taken to the 65th General Hospital near Norwich, England. Once there, another doctor examined him. It was readily determined that Bob had suffered more than just a gash on his head. After tapping repeatedly on his back, the doctor informed him, "You have a compression fracture of the T-6th, 7th, and 8th vertebrae." In layman's terms, that translated into a broken back.

Most likely, the injury occurred when Bob was finally able to get his parachute open. He was not in a vertical position when the chute jerked him upward and it deployed with a terrific jolt. Bob did not feel pain at that time, no doubt due to the trauma of his situation. Then he fell into the bitter cold arms of the North Sea, which numbed his senses. Now in the hospital, he was experiencing the discomfort of an injured back, but he was unsure of what was wrong until the doctor had informed him.

Bob was able to call his mom and dad from the hospital. He told them that they may be receiving an MIA (Missing in Action) letter, but not to worry. He explained, "I had an accident, but I'm alright. I'm in a hospital in England where they are taking care of a back injury I got."

Bob was wheeled on a gurney to an area designated for administering casts, where he remained for a few hours. He was to receive a body cast (chest to hip). A "T-shirt" was put on him as Step One of the lengthy process. It was a messy business as nurses repeatedly dipped strips of cloth into plaster then onto his chest and back.

The cast was full in the back, while the front curved up a bit from the bottom for ease of sitting, and there was a mid-chest window to make breathing easier. Bob adjusted quite well to the restriction of the full cast. Often, as time went on and he was healing, he experienced itching sensations. He found a stick that he could slip under the cast to scratch his back.

One day, Bob lit up a cigarette. After a couple of minutes, he experienced a burning warmth in his chest area. He soon realized that he had inadvertently dropped some of the ashes in the window of his cast. Squirming like crazy, he dug the ashes out. Needless to say, it never happened again. Bob remained in that body cast for more than two months.

Rehab was a requirement for Bob's recovery. He was instructed to do calisthenics on a daily basis. The doctor visited him one morning and told him to go out into the field with some of the other patients and play softball. A puzzled Bob responded, "You've got to be kidding! How am I supposed to do that?"

"Just do what you can. Go on out and move around," the doctor said in no uncertain terms. So Bob got out of his bed and walked outdoors. The sunshine and fresh air pleasantly stimulated his senses and he found that he very much enjoyed being there. As the days passed, he was able to physically do more than he expected.

Bob showing off his cast with its
mid-chest window.

George and Laura Givens stayed well-informed of their
son's injury and his road to recovery as Bob faithfully wrote
to them every day.

As the weeks passed, Bob regained his strength and his
back pain subsided. He was once permitted to go to town
with some of the other guys. He had to borrow a shirt larger
than normal for him because it had to cover his body cast.
After they arrived in town, he went along with the others
into the pub of their choice. Not long after they entered, a
girl whistled loudly and shouted to Bob, "My gosh! You've
got a good build!"

Staff Sergeant Robert Givens was back to full strength after almost three months in the body cast. He had the autographs of a lot of nurses on it (along with their addresses). When it was time to take it off, he announced, "That thing's goin' back to the States!"

Getting it off didn't take as long as he expected. Later he would recollect, "That baby was off in no time flat!"

The minute it was lifted from his body, he breathed a huge sigh of relief and declared, "Aw, keep it. I don't want to see it anymore!"

Before Bob was granted discharge from the hospital, he was required to pass a fitness test. There was only one basic requirement: he had to complete a fifteen-mile hike around the area. He and several others were sent out to an old trail that snaked around the hospital. They were required to wear heavy packs on their backs to determine their ability to be discharged with full strength and stamina. Bob thought this was good therapy. He was able to achieve it on his first attempt, and was soon on his way, good as new.

Bob Givens had earned the Purple Heart and received his medal while in the hospital in England.

16

The Last Straw

T HE "NUMBER ONE" THING ON BOB'S MIND as he left the hospital was to get back to duty. He just wanted to continue flying. He was soon assigned to another crew. Early one morning, they took off in miserable weather. It was raining and the wind was fairly strong, but this was just a practice run. They flew around the area and everything was fine — until the landing.

The pilot approached too fast and missed the beginning of the runway. The plane did not touch down until the middle and then ran off the other end, as everyone on board braced for the worst. In a split second, it raced across the grass and straight into a field of straw, where it finally came to a stop.

This was more than Bob could handle, after his last plane breaking apart and his two-mile fall into the North Sea. Then the rescue plane blew a tire upon landing, and now this incident. "That's it for me! I've had enough!" he proclaimed.

It was a rather sobering moment for the young man who loved to fly but got more than he could deal with at that time. Although he was never diagnosed officially, he felt as though he'd had "a bit of a nervous breakdown."

17

Over the Bounding Main

B OB WAS BEING SENT BACK TO THE United States. He boarded a big troop ship that was taking on a group of German soldiers as prisoners. It was Bob's first time on a ship. This was the commodore ship in a convoy of more than a dozen ships headed across the Atlantic.

In the mess hall, the American soldiers sat on one side of the table and the Germans sat on the other side. Bob was assigned to guard duty on the deck and he was given a 12-guage shotgun. All in all, the Germans were treated well aboard the ship and they were in good spirits. They were going to a new place with the opportunity for a new beginning. But Bob had no love for the Germans after what they had done during the war. He thought, *If they all jump overboard, it's ok with me.*

They had been sailing along steadily since their departure and Bob was enjoying the ride. It was with a sense of wonder that he gazed out and saw nothing but ocean. Bob was mesmerized while standing near the bow, watching the water fan furiously out to the side as the big ship cut through the waves. Equally fascinating was the wake full of bubbles and foam that trailed behind them. Also, there was a feeling of prominence being on the commodore ship ahead of the others.

One morning Bob woke up to stillness and quiet. After several days of motoring along, and with many more days to go, he felt this was very strange. It was still wartime and German subs could be anywhere. *This could be really dangerous,* he thought as he got dressed.

Another guy said, "If a German sub sees us, we're gone! We'll catch a torpedo for sure!"

The other ships in the convoy went around them and continued on their way. Bob's ship was alone—dead in the water. Apparently, there was an engine malfunction and the captain had been in contact with the other ships. It was something that could be repaired but would take a while. Meanwhile, they were very vulnerable, and very nervous. The crew's fears were warranted.

After two or three hours, everyone cheered as the engines suddenly rumbled. The captain "opened her up and gave her full gun." They caught up with the convoy and once again took the lead. Then they slowed down because they could only travel at the same speed as the slowest ship in the convoy.

Soon, Bob was feeling he was ready to get off that ship. The quarters were cramped. They were stacked with four bunks high. While some of the guys played cards, Bob didn't get into it. He was thinking, *Boy, am I glad I never got into the Navy!*

Fortunately, the weather was good throughout the crossing. It had been eleven days since they left port in England when they finally spotted the Statue of Liberty! Bob never dreamed it would look so good. A powerful symbol of freedom and welcome, it was awe-inspiring as they drew closer to it. Bob also never dreamed that he would be in New York Harbor. He was one happy young man! Back in the good ol' USA!

Some of the guys got so excited, they threw their helmets in the water, where they looked like a bunch of pots floating around. They just wanted to show how happy they were, but Bob kept his. He thought, *Only a group of GIs would do such a silly thing.*

It took a long time to enter the harbor and to line up at the pier. The troops stayed aboard while the ship was unloaded. Some were already empty, no doubt coming back for supplies. The German prisoners were sent all over the U.S., including some to Bob's home state of Minnesota.

18

The Flyboy Returns

I T WAS EARLY IN 1944 WHEN BOB WAS SENT TO Camp Kilmer, New Jersey, for a few days while the paperwork for his leave was complete. Then he was sent by train to Fort Snelling in St. Paul, Minnesota. There he was given a physical. His back was ok. After a day or two, he was heading home at last on a Greyhound bus to Duluth. He waited there for a while, then boarded one more bus headed for the Iron Range. Not having seen him for two years, his parents were anxiously waiting in Eveleth as the bus rolled in.

Barely able to contain their excitement, his mom and dad stood on the sidewalk, awaiting their son's arrival. Down Fayal Avenue came the familiar bus, which that day looked so special. It slowed down, then came to a stop in front of them. The doors separated and out stepped Staff Sergeant Robert Gordon Givens in full uniform.

Needless to say, it was an emotional and thrilling moment for all of them as they embraced and fully acknowledged that only something miraculous had brought Bob back home. They were a very close family and there was no shortage of hugs and kisses that day.

Bob had been granted a thirty-day leave, and he immediately started enjoying it. He loved to sit at the kitchen table and have conversations with his mom and dad and sometimes with the neighbors. He had missed his mother's excellent cooking and baking, and now he heartily indulged in it. He would often take out his old .22 rifle and go hunting, just as he used to do. He also did a lot of visiting with friends and neighbors and folks around town.

Soon after he returned home, Bob was aware that most of the people there had heard about his fall from the plane. He got the nickname "Two Mile" because of his harrowing 12,000-foot descent before being able to deploy his parachute. This fact was verified by the military and published in an article in the *Stars and Stripes* newspaper, which operates from within the U.S. Department of Defense. Bob was granted a 10% disability from the military due to his back injury, which amounted to a raise in his salary of around $50 a month.

The military required a soldier to wear his full uniform in public when on leave. One day Bob decided to go to the school and "show off." He wanted to visit the shop teacher, of whom he was particularly fond. They had a good visit and Bob certainly attracted a lot of attention that day among both faculty and students. On the way home, he stopped in the post office, where he was greeted with hugs and kisses from the ladies there.

Bob home on leave, ea1944.

When Bob had been sixteen, his father had bought a car, which Bob drove until he left for the service and then it was sold. Now Bob felt the need for one again, so he rented one from a neighbor for $100 a month. After a while, the guy got "antsy" about it, so Bob returned it. He had spotted a '37 Pontiac in the back of a service garage in Eveleth. It was covered with many objects and was barely visible, but the chrome caught Bob's eye.

No cars were being made during the war, as all of the steel was needed for the military. Automobiles were hard to find then, and while the Pontiac was pretty much junked, Bob bought it, fixed it up, and got it running. Then he really started enjoying himself. He did his share of drinking, dancing, and cruising around having fun while on leave.

19

AWOL—
with Good Reason

A FTER THIRTY DAYS HAD PASSED, Bob said good-by to his parents and drove the '37 Pontiac to Truax Field in Madison, Wisconsin. While there, Bob was assigned to be in charge of the supply room. This job was just something for him to do for the time being.

Two or three months before the end of the actual war, while still in Madison, Bob was with a group of fellow soldiers. For some time there had been a feeling among the troops that something was going to happen soon, yet everyone was surprised when one day the radio blasted, "They just announced victory in Europe!"

For the first time in his life, Bob went AWOL (Absent Without Leave). Several of the guys jumped into Bob's car and they headed to Milwaukee. Boy, did they have a good

Plans for V-J Day... Final Victory and a Better World

V.E. Day

Image from an unknown source showing anonymous enlisted men celebrating victory in Europe as WWII ends.

time! They were treated like kings. They couldn't buy a thing—everything was on the house. Kegs of beer kept rolling down the street for all of the soldiers.

When they returned to Truax to face their punishment, they were in for a surprise. Nothing was ever said to any of them about it. They assumed that they had earned the celebration.

In spite of VE Day (Victory in Europe,) the war was still continuing in Japan. Bob stayed at the base in Madison until June. In the meantime, he was enjoying his time in the service so much that he decided to re-enlist, this time into something dubbed "Project Wonderful," involving a group of B-29s to be used in Europe for three years.

20

Time for Romance

P RIOR TO REPORTING FOR DUTY IN 1945 on Project Wonderful, Bob was granted a ninety-day leave. He got in his '37 Pontiac and drove home to Leonidas. In short, he started "cattin' around." He was hitting the taverns, dancing, and he had a brief romance. The girl wanted to get married, but Bob was set on a military career. He thought that marriage was not yet in the cards for him.

However, his head was turned by another girl one day. While he was driving through downtown Eveleth, a pretty girl driving another car went by. With no hesitation, Bob circled around and followed her to the alley behind her home. She drove the car into the garage, and Bob drove right in behind her. "Hey — move your car! I can't shut the door!" she shouted.

With a big grin, the persistent Bob shouted back, "I will when you agree to go out with me!"

Bob once again home on leave,
late 1944.

After a brief conversation, Dolores Longar succumbed to the charms of the handsome flyboy and agreed to go out with him. That evening, Bob picked up the young lady at her house and met her mother. Dolores's parents were Slovenian and neither spoke English, so their greeting was just a smile and a nod. Dolores was the youngest of their ten children.

Bob took her to a popular tavern in Eveleth where there was a nickelodeon and a live polka band. He had learned some good dance moves from guys at Gunnery School and there was a USO Club on almost every base in the States.

The military would bring in busloads of local women so the men could meet and dance with them. Bob had plenty of dancing experience and soon found that Dolores was a good dancer as well. They had a few drinks and discovered that they both liked to dance. They just seemed to "click" and it was the first of many dates for the young couple that summer. Bob started to call her "Dorothy" simply because he liked that name better, and by the end of August, they had discussed marriage and she accepted a ring that Bob had bought for her.

21

Back to Europe

WHEN FALL ARRIVED, BOB WAS ON A TRAIN headed for a B-29 base in Clovis, New Mexico, where he would train for "Project Wonderful." He wrote letters to Dorothy every day. He was assigned to the position of "blister operator," so called because there was a Plexiglas bulge on the side of the plane where he was stationed. This position was the same as a waist gunner on a B-17. These turrets were remote-controlled and there were two men side-by-side in each of them. On his first flight, as the large aircraft lumbered down the runway, Bob asked over the radio, "Hey, doesn't this thing ever get up in the air?"

The response was, "You're not on a B-17, boy! This one takes longer." Flying around Pike's Peak, they could see tourists on the ground below. The pilot tipped the plane sideways as they flew through Devil's Gorge, and Bob could see the people watching with open mouths.

After training to be a blister operator for Project Wonderful, Bob was disappointed when the whole deal was scrubbed because the European countries and the United States could not agree on having the U.S. B-29s there for that length of time. Therefore, Project Wonderful was dissolved.

Bob got orders to report to aircraft maintenance school at Chanute Field, Illinois. It was six weeks of training and a "pretty damn good school," he admitted. He bought a '36 Ford Business Coupe with a rumble seat. Every weekend, he drove 1,200-plus miles round trip to visit his mom and dad — and his girlfriend Dorothy.

When the training ended, he was sent back to Clovis, New Mexico. While there, Bob received notice that he was to go to Germany as part of the 27th Fighter Group. The planes in this group were P-47s, with Pratt & Whitney single engines. With their double row of pistons, they had increased power and so were designed as pursuit planes to protect bombers. The complication now for Bob was that his relationship with Dorothy had deepened over the months through their letters and weekend visits, and he hated to leave her and go to overseas.

22

I Do

A S SOON AS HE WAS ABLE, BOB GOT on the telephone and called Dorothy. He had an eight-day leave before going to Germany and he had plans for how he wanted to spend that time. Shortly after he arrived back home, he picked up Dorothy and they drove to Veterans' Park at Ely Lake, where he wasted no time in asking her to marry him. Bob said, "Don't worry. I'll get you over there." She said yes.

However, there was another problem. Bob's parents were staunch Protestants and Dorothy was raised Catholic. Religious differences were the cause of a great many foiled marriages and family rejection in those days. George and Laura Givens liked Dorothy enough to give their blessing for Bob to marry a Catholic.

And so, on November 1, 1946, Bob and Dorothy went to visit the priest at the Resurrection Catholic Church in Eveleth. There were several stipulations that must be met in order for a non-Catholic to marry in the church, including a training session that lasted many weeks. Also, Bob was against changing his religion. The odds were not in his favor.

Bob pleaded with the priest, "I have good parents, I went to Sunday school through the 11th grade, and I believe in the good Lord. Dorothy and I want to get married right away. I am shipping out for Germany in a week and I don't have time for lectures and lessons. Oh—and I do not want to change my religion."

"I see," replied the priest after what seemed a long pause. "Will you promise to raise all children that you may have together as Catholic?"

"Yes. Yes I will," responded Bob.

The priest went on to explain that it was against the church rules for them to marry in the church, but he could do it in the parish house next door. Happily, they agreed to return later that day for the ceremony. Dorothy's sister and her husband stood up for them and Mr. and Mrs. Robert Givens left the parish house. They went to the Androy Hotel in the nearby town of Hibbing for their wedding night.

Bob and Dorothy (Longar) on their wedding
day, November 1, 1946.

To Germany - and Beyond

T HE FOLLOWING WEEK, BOB LEFT HIS WIFE in Eveleth and he boarded a train headed for Camp Kilmer, New Jersey, where he spent a day or two as paperwork was completed. This time, he was crossing the ocean in a general ship instead of a big troop ship. It was considerably better since in the quarters, the men were not stacked up like cordwood. On this ship they were spread out more. Bob was a staff sergeant by then and he was assigned private quarters.

Walking on the deck one day, he heard, "Hi, Bob!" It was a guy he had gone to school with in Leonidas when they were young. Bill was working for the government, not the military. The crossing went more quickly as they often met to catch up on each other's life and experiences since they had left home.

A week or so later, the ship pulled into Bremerhaven, Germany. As they debarked the ship, they were met by trucks that transported the men to the base. Bob never saw Bill again.

Fritzler, Germany was a former Luftwaffe base. Their planes shot down Allied planes during the war. Fritzler was now the headquarters of the U.S. 27th fighter group.

Raw winter winds laced with snow blasted their faces at Fritzler and Bob felt right at home, having been raised in northern Minnesota. The base was fifteen to twenty miles from Kassel, Germany, which was a fair-sized town that had been heavily bombed by the RAF and by U.S. bombers as well. Therefore, no housing was available outside of the base, and wives were not allowed to stay at the base. Bob and his crew had helped destroy the housing that he now needed for himself and his new wife. Much to their dismay, Dorothy was forced to stay at home.

It was late November 1946 and Bob was a crew chief. He eventually worked his way up to the position of line chief, in charge of several aircraft parked in a line on the field. Pilots would practice flying with twenty-seven planes in formation. Once back on the ground, the pilots made note of anything they observed that was wrong with the plane during the flight.

The pilots' notes were given to the crew chief on the ground. The chief would see to it that repair or replacement took place. Bob did this job for two months.

With little notice, the 27th fighter group was abolished. Some guys were sent back to the states. Bob was sent to Pisa, Italy by train and he enjoyed the scenic ride on the way there. At the base in Pisa, all of the aircraft housed there were DC- airliners from the European Air Transport Service. The military called them C-47s, and they were the "freight cars of the Air Force." They had been used to transport troops and supplies during the war. Bob was the ground crew chief on one of them. For a few months he inspected, maintained, washed, cleaned, and greased the plane.

Then the orders came to shut down the entire operation in Pisa.

24

Moving On

B OB WAS ON ANOTHER TRAIN, THIS time headed for
Leghorn, Italy. There he boarded a ship (the *General
Richardson*) crossed the Mediterranean Sea, passed through
the Straights of Gibraltar, and once again crossed the Atlantic.

As soon as he got off the ship in New York Harbor, Bob
searched for the nearest telephone and called his wife. When
the phone rang at the Longar home in Eveleth, Minnesota
that day, a delighted Mrs. Robert Givens answered. Happy
to have her husband back on U.S. soil, she could hardly wait
to see him again. Bob got on the next train and headed home.

Dorothy was living with her parents in Eveleth and a joyful
reunion took place when Bob arrived. He had a two-week
leave and they stayed there at her parents' home, although
he spent plenty of time with his parents, friends, and family
as well. He needed another car so he purchased a '39
Oldsmobile sedan.

When his leave was up, Bob was ordered to report to the air base at Kearney, Nebraska. This time he was able to take Dorothy with him and they drove there together. They stayed in an old Army barracks building that had been divided into five apartments. They remained there until a more suitable place was available.

A staff sergeant was allowed "rations" and "quarters" (Basic Allowance Subsistence). Even so, by the end of the month, their budget was always stretched and Bob and Dorothy ate Mrs. Grass's soup often (a dry soup mix to which water is added). Inexpensive and filling, it often sustained them until Bob got his next paycheck.

25

A Time of Sorrow

A COUPLE OF MONTHS PASSED, AND BOB'S group got orders to report to gunnery practice at McDill Field in Tampa, Florida. It was especially difficult for Bob to leave this time because Dorothy was pregnant with their first child. Since he was only expected to be gone for ninety days, she stayed in Kearney. Many other GI wives were there and she was accustomed to living in their apartment, plus there was a car available for her use.

Bob left by train for Tampa, where it was so hot that when working on the P-51s, guys would sometimes burn their hands. He was there for a few weeks when he got a phone call from Dorothy. She was having problems with the pregnancy and had taken the train back to Duluth.

Concerned for Dorothy's well-being and that of their unborn child, Bob rushed to the Red Cross and explained the situation. The Red Cross made a few calls and determined that she was in the hospital. Then Bob went to the commanding officer (CO) of the base and described his dilemma. The CO made some calls himself and found that Dorothy had been released from the hospital, but he told Bob to go home anyway and take care of his wife.

As soon as possible, Bob jumped on a train back to Kearney, got his car, and drove to Eveleth. Dorothy was with her parents in Eveleth and feeling better. After a week or so, she felt fine and they drove back to Nebraska.

****

It was 1948 and Bob was close to the end of his three-year enlistment. Even though his time was not completely up, he was qualified for a "Dependent Discharge" due to the fact that he and Dorothy were expecting a child.

So, Bob was officially discharged from the service and he and Dorothy drove back to Eveleth. Soon after, she went into labor and an excited yet nervous Bob awaited the birth.

The doctor came out to deliver the devastating news. Their newborn son was a "blue baby" (a symptom of a heart defect resulting from a lack of oxygen in the blood supply).

The child died two days later.

26

The Family Man

T HE COUPLE ONCE AGAIN MOVED IN with Dorothy's mom and dad in Eveleth. Bob needed to find a job and he didn't have to look far. The Oliver Mining Company in that town hired him on the spot.

The government had a program at that time called the "50/20 Club." A discharged serviceman could get $20 every week for fifty-two weeks. Bob figured that since he now had a job, he would save the 50/20 for an emergency cushion later. Therefore, he never signed up for it. Eventually, the program was dissolved and Bob lost out on the $1,040 he could have collected.

After a month or so of working at the Oliver mine, the foreman walked over to Bob and said, "You gotta stay home for a while."

"Why? What did I do?" a worried Bob asked.

The foreman smiled and explained, "You have two weeks of vacation coming. You worked here before you went into the service and the government requires us to count your six years. You have over six years of rights comin', so you get two weeks off." Bob enjoyed staying home and taking it easy for a while.

Eventually he got a better car. His uncle died and his aunt did not drive. Bob's Aunt Sue gave him a 1940 Pontiac that was like brand new. By then he and Dorothy were renting a small apartment in Eveleth. She was pregnant again and this time a healthy son was born on December 5, 1949. They named him Greg.

27

Return to Duty

T HE NATIONAL GUARD HAD A DIVISION IN Eveleth and Bob was asked to join. He agreed and entered as a supply sergeant. They had meetings at least once a month at the Eveleth Armory and he enjoyed being part of a military organization again. He reported to Camp Ripley near Brainerd, Minnesota for two weeks every summer.

In the fall of 1950, talk of a Korean War was in the wind. Word got around that the National Guard was going to be federalized. As the rumors increased, Bob realized that he had put himself in the position of being called back to active duty. Without hesitation, he went to the C.O. and requested a transfer out of the National Guard and back into the Air Force. It was approved. Bob got a letter two weeks later welcoming him back into the Air Force. It was January of 1951.

Once again having to leave his wife and son, Bob reported for duty, this time in Rapid City, South Dakota, where there

Bob returns to active duty, early 1951.

was a big B-36 bomber base. A day and a half later, he was re-assigned to Moses Lake, Washington with the 27th fighter group as an instrument technician. These were different planes than the B-17s he had flown on before. The P-47s (called "Jugs") were shorter and faster. They were one of the first planes to break the speed of sound. Now they also had jets — F-86 fighter jets. Bob was excited about them.

Meanwhile, Dorothy was packing up and having furniture shipped to Moses Lake, which was paid for by the military.

Bob had rented a small apartment in the Wherry Housing Project, which was mostly military. Their rent was $75 a month, which still stretched their budget, so Bob got a job waiting on tables at the NCO Club, to help cover their expenses.

After only two months, Bob was ordered to ship out. Exasperated, he said to the CO, "I just got my wife and son out here! Can't it wait a couple of months?"

The CO replied, "Geez, Bob, this one's goin' to England. The next one's probably goin' to Korea. You'll be part of NATO if you go now." Bob elected to go to England.

After saying goodbye to his wife and young son, Bob, and the entire 27th fighter group, was shipped to Ipswich, England. They were there as part of NATO, as the CO had told Bob. Their mission was to keep peace in Europe. Bob was assigned to an instrument shop and there he worked with a different kind of crew. They were "young bloods," just kids, really. Bob lived on the base and was no longer the "new kid on the block."

28

Life Changes

B OB WAS IN ENGLAND FOR OVER A YEAR. At that time, the rule was that if you were married, your family could not live there with you. In November of '51, they passed a rule that if you were married and desired to leave the service, you could. Since there was no housing for his wife and child, Bob qualified and he opted out of the service once again to join his family. He left by ship from Liverpool to New York (his last trip past the Statue of Liberty.) From there, he took a train to McGuire Air Force Base, where he was formally discharged.

Later on, the "Homestead Act" was passed. This allowed an enlisted man's wife and children to live on base with him for a period of three years. Bob would have stayed in the service had that been the case. In the meantime, his wife had arranged to leave the baby with her mother and was on her way to meet him. They were looking forward to

Bob is formally discharged from the service, November, 1951.

settling down at last. But first, they were going to see New York City together.

When Dorothy arrived, they happily explored the city, including Chinatown, the Empire State Building, and even skating in Rockefeller Center. It was close to Christmas in 1951. They went to Grand Central Station and took a train back home.

Bob was given a job again at the Oliver Mining Company. He was a production truck driver and sometimes a mechanic's helper in the shops. He would steam clean parts and determine what was wrong with them. He also re-joined the National Guard. They rented a house in Eveleth until Dorothy's mother died. Dorothy's father, Frank Longar, was unaccustomed to living alone and did not cook for himself, so Bob, Dorothy, and the baby moved in with him.

A daughter was born on November 18, 1952. She was named Laura after Bob's mother.

They stayed with Dorothy's father until 1955 when they bought a house in Midway, which was close by. The following year, another son was born and they named him Glenn.

Bob remained in the National Guard until 1958. There was a strike expected at the Oliver mine. At that time, there was an opening for a custodian at the Virginia, Minnesota School District, close to Bob's home. There were many who interviewed for the job, but Bob got it. He quit working for the mining company after sixteen years and began a new career.

He started out with the maintenance crew, and later that year he began as an emergency bus driver. Between bus runs, he cleaned the band hall and the auto mechanics shop. Now he was a full-time employee, earning full-time pay and benefits, although it was considerably less than he had earned at the mining company. However, he felt that his family needed the security of a steady paycheck, which he got from the school district.

For a man with wartime military experience, driving a school bus may have seemed like a walk in the park. However, it was not without its challenges, as Bob soon discovered. He was assigned to a bus that was populated with several notoriously ill-behaved riders, and no one else wanted it.

Bob relied on what he knew best in order to keep them in line. When former Staff Sergeant Robert Givens took the wheel of that bus, military order took place. He laid down the new rules, plain and simple: girls on one side, boys on the other. The bus was loaded like a troop train. Girls first, three-to-a-seat, back to front; then boys, the same way.

Bob admitted that he "didn't put up with any crap." He watched the mirror as much as possible and when there was a problem, he would stop the bus, get up, and shout, "Any more of that and you're out the door! Nobody asked you to get on this bus. This is the way it's gonna be." He didn't have to do that very many times before his charges realized this guy meant what he said.

His main concern was for the safety of the children. Bob laid down the law and they came to respect him for that. But he became more than a strict bus driver to them. If he could do a favor for a kid, Bob would go out of his way to do it.

As the years went by, he often drove the bus on athletic trips, where he would frequently sit on the bench with the kids. For the sports-minded bus driver, Bob loved this and got along with them very well. Bob was admittedly strict with his own children also. Years later, his oldest son thanked him for being strict and raising them well.

On January 14, 1959, another son was born and he was named Geoffrey. Six years later, he started school and Dorothy was thinking about getting a job. She had taken shorthand and typing in high school and would be able to work as a secretary.

She first was hired part-time by an elderly attorney in Eveleth. After a couple of years, she was offered a full-time position with an attorney at a firm in Virginia, Minnesota, and in 1975 a different firm in Virginia asked her boss to join them. He agreed and asked Dorothy to go with him. With hard work and dedicated service, she worked her way up to the position of paralegal.

29

Good Times

I N ADDITION TO THEIR LOVE OF DANCING, Bob and Dorothy shared the enjoyment of camping and fishing. Bob would say, "Are we gonna go camping for the weekend?"

Dorothy would happily respond, "I'd love to!"

The next day the car would be all packed up and the family would be ready to go. Bob bought a boat that he named "Rogue," and there were many years of fun weekend trips to Crane Lake, Minnesota.

Eventually, they purchased a 14'x72', three-bedroom mobile home and moved it to the Red Carpet Resort, further north. This resort was on the Rainy River in Baudette, Minnesota, at the entrance to strikingly beautiful Lake of the Woods. They burned a trail (176 miles each way) from their home in Midway, Minnesota to their wilderness fun spot, where the fishing was always "pretty damn good!" as Bob said.

It had been a dream of Bob and Dorothy's to have a get-away place of their own, a place where they could retire. They hoped to spend winters down south somewhere and summers in Baudette. Their entire family looked forward to going there as much as possible.

Bob retired from the school district at the age of sixty after twenty-six years. The "Rule of '85" allowed employees to retire with full benefits when their age plus their years of service to the district equaled eighty-five. Bob qualified in 1984 and he took the deal.

Dorothy continued working for the law firm in Virginia and was able to work three-day weeks, taking off Fridays and Mondays. They enjoyed long weekends in Baudette.

****

Bob and Dorothy had long dreamed about taking a vacation to Hawaii. In 1989, they decided to go. This was Bob's first trip on a commercial airliner and it was a completely different flying experience than he was used to. Bob readily admitted it was really nice and that he enjoyed it very much. Sitting back and relaxing on a plane while it casually transported you halfway across the Pacific Ocean was a very pleasant experience for him. Part-way through the flight, Bob got up and strolled to the front of the plane. The cockpit door was open and he addressed the pilot and the co-pilot with a friendly, "Hi, guys! Can an old B-17 boy take a look?"

They swerved around and the pilot responded in surprise, "You were on a B-17? Come right in!" Bob got a tour of the cockpit.

The Bob Givens Family. *Front, L-R*: Geoffrey, Bob, Shawn the dog, Dorothy, Glenn. *Back, L-R*: Greg, Laura.

Bob and Dorothy were staying for one week in Waikiki at the Pagoda Hotel (aka the Iron Range Hotel since a Virginia, Minnesota travel agency booked many visitors there.) They had planned to take a helicopter tour of all five islands, but it was too windy. Instead, they bought a bus pass and went all over the island of Oahu. They could walk to the beach from the Pagoda Hotel. They took several tours and saw Diamondhead, Chinaman's Hat, a pineapple plantation, and the Veterans' cemetery. While at the USS *Arizona*, they noticed the name "Givens" on the roster of men lost there during the attack on Pearl Harbor, although he was no relation to Bob.

They were having a wonderful vacation. Bob said it was a was a "fun, happy, sweet time" for them. After they returned home, Dorothy mentioned that she had experienced some headaches while they were in Hawaii.

30

A Devastating Loss

TWO OF DOROTHY'S SEVEN SISTERS HAD breast cancer. Then she got it. She did not have surgery because she was experiencing very bad headaches. Bob took her to Duluth, where doctors performed a spinal tap. The news got worse. They discovered the cancer was also in her brain. The doctor in Duluth asked if they were willing to go to the NIH (National Institute of Health) in Bathesda, Maryland to try out a new drug. Bob and Dorothy agreed. Their insurance paid for the flight and the week-long stay.

Dorothy was the first or second person in the country to try the new drug. However, she and Bob were soon informed that it had not worked. Still reeling from this news, they were then given the prognosis. She had only a few weeks or months to live. While they were both in a state of shock, on the way home from Bathesda, Dorothy had a seizure in the airport. When she recovered, they knew they had to get back and tell their children.

Not an easy thing to do, they did so as soon as they arrived home, and they tried their best to deal with the shock and sorrow of their children, family, and friends. While she never seemed to experience great pain, Dorothy did suffer severe seizures, and four to five weeks after they returned from Bathesda, she was in hospice at the Eveleth Hospital. Bob had brought her there on the morning of September 25, 1990 because she had gotten progressively weaker every day. She was not in much pain at that time and death did not seem imminent, so after several hours, Bob left her for a while in the company of their daughter Laura.

Dorothy quietly passed away that evening.

Bob was at such a loss. The questions, "Why did you have to take her?" and, "Why not me?"were uttered in his despair. Yet, because he had witnessed so many of her seizures and her increasing weakness, he knew he had to let her go.

After a while, believing that she was in a better place and free from suffering, he humbled himself and uttered the words, "Thank you, Lord, for taking her." After the funeral, the husband of one of her sisters said, "Well, Bob, now Dorothy is on the Lord's legal staff!" Even Bob had to chuckle at that thought.

Wrestling with his loneliness and the loss of the woman he had so dearly loved and been married to for forty-four years, Bob felt like an exile in his own world. He could not imagine how his life could go on from there.

Two long, miserable years passed. Then one day, he wandered into Sammy's, a local tavern in Virginia, Minnesota.

31

A Second Chance

S AMMY'S WAS A POPULAR GATHERING place with live music, a good dance floor, and they poured a good drink. Bob sat on a stool at the bar, as he often did. Then the door opened and in walked a "good-lookin' chick" he had never seen before. She was with two other women, but Bob definitely perked up at the sight of the first one. They came in, and as luck would have it, they chose to sit at the bar, not far away from Bob.

Before long, he flashed a smile and motioned to that good-lookin' chick asking, "Wanna dance?" She nodded her head and they walked out to the dance floor. That was the first of many dances to come. Her name was Opal and she had come in with her brother's wife and a girlfriend.

After that first meeting, Bob and Opal were often seen driving around a lot, dancing, and enjoying drinks. She laughed often, and she liked to travel. Bob had come back to life and was beginning to think that maybe he could find happiness again. He went to the boyfriend of Opal's girlfriend and asked him what kind of girl Opal really was.

"You got no problem there, Bob. She's a good girl," he stated without hesitation.

Opal, who was then divorced, had three children with her former husband. She had a nice home in central Virginia, Minnesota.

They had been dating for six months when Bob admitted to the fact that he needed someone. Opal was a pretty girl, kind and fun to be with. He was smitten for the second time in his life.

When he asked her to marry him, she said, "Yes! Let's go to Las Vegas!" Her girlfriend Mabel and the boyfriend Bob had questioned about Opal, went with them. They stayed at the Union Plaza Hotel and on April 7, 1992, they had a double-wedding ceremony. Bob remarked, "It was very nice," and they stayed there for a couple of days.

The military had sent Bob Givens all over the United States as well as several places in Europe before, during, and after World War II. But the flyboy from Leonidas wasn't finished traveling. He discovered that in Opal, he not only found a second chance at love, but much more than that. She kept a neat house, was always concerned about his health, made delicious pork and beef roasts, and a wonderful stew, among other things. She took "pretty darned good care of me," he admitted. And she turned out to be a great travel partner.

One of the first trips they took after their marriage was a twenty-five-day excursion to Australia, New Zealand, Fiji,

Bob marries Opal in Las Vegas, April 7, 1992.

and Hawaii. The next year, they decided to escape the Minnesota winter and go to Arizona for a few months. They drove there and rented a house in a town called Page. Friends later told them they would probably like Lake Havasu City better because the climate was warmer. The following year, they tried it there and liked it so much that they returned every year for seven consecutive years. Each year, they extended their stay until they remained from January through May. They visited many places while there, including the Grand Canyon and the Four Corners.

When it became too much for them to drive to Arizona every year, they started taking bus tours all over the United States. One thirty-day trip took them to New England, through Montreal, Nova Scotia, and other parts of Canada, the St. Lawrence Seaway, Cape Cod, and Pennsylvania.

On another tour, they headed to west to California, where they saw the *Queen Mary* docked in Long Beach, the famous Howard Hughes's plane called the *Spruce Goose*, San Diego, Los Angeles, and the Danish town of Solvang.

Branson, Missouri was the destination for two other trips they took, including one at Christmas time.

Then Bob got stopped in his tracks.

32

A Stroke of Luck

H EALTH CHALLENGES SOMETIMES OCCUR before we are aware of any symptoms. During a routine vision exam in 1990, a malignant tumor was discovered in the optic nerve of Bob's left eye. The tumor was removed and the doctor told Bob he would gradually lose his vision in that eye. Five years passed before he was blind in his left eye.

Twelve years later, Bob had been having symptoms suggesting that something was physically wrong with him. When the doctor examined him, he discovered that his left kidney was in such bad shape that it had to be removed. On May 8, 2007, Bob was taken to Duluth for the surgery, which went well.

Opal, along with her son and his wife, had gone out for a quick meal since they had been told that the surgery had been a success and that Bob would be in recovery for some time. His daughter, Laura, had returned to her home about thirty miles away. The hospital staff did not know where to locate Opal if necessary, which soon became the case. Bob had a stroke while in the recovery room.

The hospital contacted Laura at her home and she called Opal, who had just arrived back at the hotel, informing her of what had occurred. It was a shock since Opal had been under the impression that Bob was fine. She and her son and daughter-in-law came rushing back to the Intensive Care Unit. If one is going to have a stroke, there is no better place to have one than in a hospital. Bob was given immediate attention, which was fortunate.

The stroke affected his left side. His arm and leg were not working and his speech also had been affected. After a day or so, he was moved to Miller Dwan Hospital in Duluth, where he felt he received "the best therapy anywhere." Two weeks, later, Opal was still staying there with him and he was progressing well. He asked to be transferred to the Virginia Hospital and get therapy there because Opal could then stay at home rather than a hotel, and it was arranged.

Bob's speech was the first thing to come back. Writing was a challenge and he had to practice as if he were writing a letter to someone. He also worked with a fellow who specialized in the area of memory. After talking with Bob for several sessions, he marveled and said, "Bob, you've got a really good memory!"

Walking was difficult and Bob had to practice walking between two bars and then up and down the stairs. All of the bedrooms in Opal's house where they had been living were upstairs. So they decided to sell the house and move into an apartment. They offered it furnished, and when Bob was able, they moved to nearby Washington Manor Apartments.

Four months later, Bob was getting better every day and

the house had not yet sold. He and Opal decided they may be able to move back, which is what they wanted to do. They called the realtor, took the house off the market, and moved back home.

A thankful Bob recovered amazingly well from the stroke and lived for more than twenty years in that same house with Opal. This may not have happened due to the fact that in 1995, the couple realized they were drinking too much. His wife stopped drinking and gave him the ultimatum: "It's either me or the bottle!"

Bob chose Opal and gratefully admitted, "I'd be dead without her."

33

In Retrospect

N EARLY NINE DECADES PASSED SINCE Robert Gordon Givens was born in a small town in northern Minnesota. He said he thought of his past seven days a week. Many of the experiences of his early life enriched him in a variety of ways and prepared him for the challenges he met as the years went by.

As an only child, he received total devotion and love from his parents. They provided every opportunity for their son to explore music, sports of many kinds, hunting, fishing, organizations, summer camps, and religion. From his parents, he learned about love, discipline, and respect.

Bob had many friends and he developed an early fascination with airplanes in a club with a group of neighborhood boys. This was his first exposure to group dynamics outside of the classroom with his peers. Cooperation and sharing of ideas were important in this early experience. Along with his best friend Wilbur, he learned to value trust and companionship.

Hunting and fishing were often the pastimes of young Bob Givens. He loved being in the woods or on the water with his dad or a couple of the neighbors. He was taught to make up his own mind and to make his own decisions, and he came to appreciate the peace and quiet of nature.

The Boy Scouts was an organization that Bob enjoyed very much. Again, the group dynamics were at work. The skills he mastered while in the Scouts served him well later in life. It was at Camp Chicagami that he learned to swim and that gave him an invaluable gift—confidence in the water.

Bob also gained confidence in the field of sports. He was good at hockey, but even better at basketball. Most of all, he excelled at football. All of these were reinforcing discipline, training, competition, and functioning in a group.

His first jobs at the Oliver mine, the CCC, and the railroad once more reiterated the importance of working with others, but they also taught him something new. He was becoming a man and it was time to stand on his own two feet, to pay his own bills, and to feel a sense of pride in doing so.

His military career was a dream-come-true for Bob. His color-blindness dashed his hopes of piloting a plane, but he didn't give up on his dream and it didn't stop him from becoming a top turret gunner. He left the small town of Leonidas, Minnesota, and traveled all over the United States during his many months of training for the military in various camps and bases. It broadened his horizons as he experienced the vast differences in the land itself and the way people live from Florida to Texas to the state of Washington and several places in-between. Later, he would also travel to several locations in Europe during his tours of duty.

All of the group dynamics Bob had experienced in his early life rose to the top of the list of importance when he became part of the Air Corps. Discipline was hammered into the recruits from Day One, but Bob was already used to that, and he respected it.

Neatness, adaptation, learning new skills, physical fitness, and leadership would all follow. Most of all, recruits were instilled with a sense of pride in the privilege of serving their country. In 1942, World War II had begun and for the U.S. forces, the provocation of this war justified their involvement.

For Bob, that sense of pride went deep, and he took it seriously. Serving on a B-17 bomber during the war required commitment, and Bob Givens had it. As a gunner, he was well-aware of the importance of his position.

Survival training became of the utmost importance when Bob's plane went down over the North Sea. Never thinking about imminent death, he concentrated on trying to get his parachute open after falling more than 12,000 feet without it. Hurtling into the icy water, Bob struggled to reach the surface. The swimming lessons he had many years before suddenly came to the forefront for his survival. He gave the utmost credit to the Boy Scouts for instilling in him confidence in the water and ultimately saving his life as he awaited rescue in the choppy, frigid waters of the North Sea. Bob also turned to his faith while he was treading water and he prayed to God that he would be saved so he could get back home to his mom and dad.

Patience was the next thing Bob was forced to learn as he was placed in a body cast after he broke his back during that horrific fall when his plane broke apart. He adapted quite well and when his therapy and recovery were complete, he felt a deep sense of appreciation for the doctors, nurses, and therapists who had cared for him.

From his romance with Dorothy and their subsequent forty-four years of marriage, Bob learned about the meaning of true love and devotion. Their children brought them an entirely new level of love. The mobile home they bought near Lake of the Woods and their trip to Hawaii were dreams-come-true for them and Bob cherished the memories of that time they spent together in both places. His great despair when Dorothy passed away was something he struggled with but eventually he came to accept it and to deal with the loss.

Then Opal came into his life and gave Bob a second chance at love. They danced a lot and enjoyed cocktails, and they traveled to many places. When drinking became a problem, they quit after an ultimatum from Opal. Bob admired her greatly for that afterward. He had come to appreciate her in a whole new way and he learned the value of compromise from her. Their marriage lasted over twenty years.

Bob's career as a school bus driver was another lesson in discipline, but this time the shoe was on the other foot. It was his turn to teach it to others, namely the rowdy students on his designated bus run. He taught them well and they came to respect him.

A malignant tumor on his optic nerve was removed and gradually caused the loss of sight in Bob's left eye. He adjusted very well to the loss of vision in that eye and it became his "new normal." He continued to do almost everything he did before except that Opal took on the responsibility of driving their car.

At least four times in his life, Bob cheated death. First, he fell 12,000 feet out of a broken plane during WWII without the use of his parachute over the North Sea. When he finally got it to open, it injured his back and he pierced the frigid water feet-first, then struggled mightily to reach the surface. Alone in the midst of the plane's debris, he was rescued minutes before hypothermia or drowning most certainly would have claimed him.

Second, he survived the landing of a plane that ran off the runway and could easily have crashed in a field when it finally came to a nerve-shattering stop.

Next, the ship transporting him back to the States went dead in the water when the engines failed in that area of the Atlantic. They were an easy target for torpedoes. Bob was again spared when the engines were repaired and they proceeded, undetected by the enemy.

Suffering a stroke after surgery for a kidney removal at the age of eighty-three, Bob once more survived and again found himself in therapy and rehab. Reminiscent of the three months he had spent in the hospital in England, while in a body cast for his injured back, he faced it with courage and determination. The bullies who long ago tried to break his spirit only succeeded in making him stronger. Bob was optimistic, believing he could overcome the obstacles that faced him, no matter how life-threatening they may be. He had proven that more than once.

When he relived the events of his life in his own mind, as he often did, Bob was proud of a successful life, a life well-lived. He was proud of the choices he made in joining the military and he took great pride in his service to his country, especially during time of war. The choices he made in the two women he married were also a matter of great satisfaction and pride to him, as were his children.

As he neared ninety years of age, a still-vital Robert Gordon Givens was certainly blessed. He felt so fortunate to have survived several life-threatening situations and to have lived as long as he did. Along the way, he learned a great many of life's lessons. He maintained a strong sense of pride and love—for his country. his family, and himself.

Bob Givens at 89 years old, proudly displaying his Air Medal and his Purple Heart, March 2013. Bob also received the Bronze Star, the American Theater Ribbon, The European Theater Ribbon, and the World War II Victory Medal. He participated in battles and campaigns in Chateaudan, France; Achmer, Rostock, and Ludwigshafen, Germany; and Courulles, Belgium.

"I have been a lucky man. Every night I thank God for all of my blessings, and I hope the good Lord will accept me into Heaven one day so I can thank him personally for the wonderful life I have had."

— *Robert G Givens*

Inspiration and Disclaimer

I N THE SMALL NORTHERN MINNESOTA TOWN known as
Virginia, the main street is lined with brick buildings
more than a century old. One of the central buildings is the
VFW, otherwise known as "the Servicemen's Club." As their
numbers have dwindled over the years, a close-knit group
of steadfast men have dedicated themselves to preserving
the dignity and upkeep of the building. Increasing taxes and
utilities over the years have brought them to the brink of
closure. In a valiant attempt to avoid this, they decided to
serve meals for a fee to the public. A leader emerged who
ably took control of the kitchen, and a dozen or so volunteers
have assisted him (most of whom are in their seventies or
eighties,) in the complete preparation of five-course meals
once or often twice a week. This has been a tradition for many
years, and the meals at the Servicemen's Club are nothing
short of delectable.

I have frequented the club along with friends and family,
and in doing so, heard people speak of a veteran from the
community who had fallen out of an airplane during World

War II and who was currently living in that same town. It occurred to me that if he were able to talk about his life experience, it would be a good story. I contacted Bob Givens in February of 2013, and he said he would be honored to meet with me.

So began my journey into the life of a man who, at eighty-nine years of age, never faltered in his recollection of events, dates, places, or people who played major roles in his development from childhood to teen, to young man, to marriage and father of four, through tragedy, and into his golden years.

Bob proudly recalled his life as he relayed it to me, and the events, dates, places, and people mentioned in this book are based on his memory of all of them. Any errors that may exist in their mention are purely unintentional.

Bob Givens passed away in December of 2013.

Appendix

The following pages contain miscellaneous documents and images related to Bob Givens' military career.

Letter home, May 20, 1944, England: "Dear Mom & Dad. Well Mom I made the Stars & Stripes over here and that's the top paper in (E.T.O.) European Theatre of War. I sent the clipping to Aunt Margo to give to you. All the fellows here are bringing in the clippings to have me autograph them. Makes me feel pretty big shot. They can't figure out yet how I'm alive today. Love always, Rob."

Falls 2 Miles Pulling In 'Detached' Chute, Then Lands in Sea

A U.S. GENERAL HOSPITAL, May 16—S/Sgt. Robert Givens, of Leonard, Minn., Eighth AF top turret gunner, is recovering from injuries after surviving a series of almost incredible escapes from death, including a 12,000-foot plunge through the air before his parachute opened, and an hour in the North Sea.

On his sixth mission over Germany, Givens' bomber stalled and went into a vertical spin, pinning him to his seat. Givens couldn't jump, but when the plane came apart in the air he was catapulted out. Upon regaining consciousness, Givens discovered that his unopened parachute had been detached from his chest, was overhead and out of reach and fastened to the loosened straps of his harness.

By pulling in the harness straps, hand over hand, as he dropped, Givens finally reached the rip cord and pulled it after descending about 12,000 feet. The sudden opening of the 'chute injured his back, and he suffered from exposure from the hour he spent in the North Sea before he was picked up by a patrol boat of the British Air/Sea Rescue Service.

Article in *Stars and Stripes* concerning Bob's fall to earth from two miles up.

CATERPILLAR CLUB

IRVING AIR CHUTE CO., INC.

1670 Jefferson Avenue
BUFFALO 8, N. Y.

Oct. 23, 1944.

S/Sgt. R. G. Givens,
Box 28,
Leoneth, Minn.

Dear Sir:

Congratulations on your recent emergency parachute jump! It is indeed gratifying to know that parachutes are daily serving their purpose and proving their worth.

We are pleased to inform you that your experience entitles you to membership in the Caterpillar Club, and we are accordingly enrolling your name on the roster of the Club.

The Irving Air Chute Company has sponsored this Club since its inception twenty years ago, and it is our endeavor to maintain our records as complete and authentic as possible. You may be interested in knowing that there are thousands of members enrolled in this Club, which lists persons from all over the world. The war, of course, has greatly increased the membership rolls which now include personnel in training in the States, and those who used their parachutes in combat areas, as well as hundreds of pilots and their crews who have baled out over enemy territory and subsequently been taken prisoners of war.

In connection with our records, therefore, we would appreciate receiving additional information relative to the incident, which may be submitted in the form of a newspaper clipping or an affidavit of a witness, together with a short personal account giving particularly your reactions and impressions of the jump.

It is also our custom to present to each new member the official insignia of the Club, engraved with his name and the date of his emergency jump. We are having your pin made and engraved, and shall forward it to you when completed, together with the membership card of the Club. Please advise date of jump.

We await further word from you with interest and welcome you into the Caterpillar Club.

Very truly yours,

IRVING AIR CHUTE CO., INC.

G. C. Krull

GCK/MMD

Invitation from the Irving Air Chute Company of Buffalo, New York, for Bob Givens to join the Caterpillar Club, whose members used their parachutes in training or combat.

The "Mae West" vest was the first inflatable life preserver, invented in 1928 by Peter Marcus. Its nickname came about because when inflated, it resembled the famous feature of the buxom actress. This letter was written by Mae West in 1942 to members of the Royal Air Force (RAF).

Dear Boys of the RAF:

I have just seen that RAF flyers have a life-saving jacket they call a "Mae West" because it bulges in all the "right places." Well, I consider it a swell honor to have such great guys wrapped up in me, know what I mean?

Yes, it's kind of a nice thought to be flying all over with brave men, even if I'm only there by proxy in the form of a life-saving jacket, or a life-saving jacket in my form. I always thought that the best way to hold a man was in your arms—but I guess when you're in the air a plane is safer. You've got to keep everything under control.

Yeah, the jacket idea is all right and I can't imagine anything better than to bring you boys of the RAF soft and happy landings. But what I'd like to know about that life-saving jacket is—has it got shapely shoulders? If I do get into the dictionary—where they say you want to put me—how will they describe me? As a warm and clinging life-saving garment worn by aviators? Or an aviator's jacket that supplies the woman's touch while the boys are flying around nights? How would you describe me boys? I've been in Who's Who and I know what's what, but it'll be the first time I ever made the dictionary.

Thanks boys.

Sin-sationally,

Mae West

Bob is honorably discharged from military service on December 5, 1945.

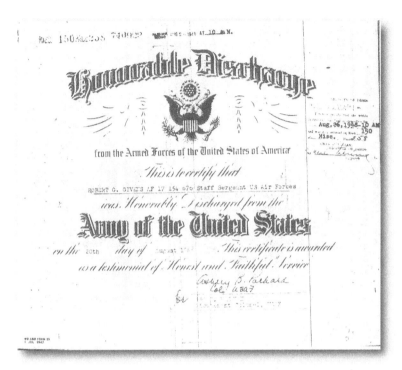

Bob receives a second honorable discharge from the Armed Forces, August 20, 1948.

Bob Givens's life membership card for the Minnesota Chapter of the Eighth Air Force Historical Society.

Bob Givens was one of over 100 veterans and 50 guardians who were privileged to participate in the Honor Flight from Duluth, Minnesota, to Washington, D.C., on May 14, 2011. Honor Flight is a non-profit organization whose purpose is to honor the sacrifices and service of veterans by providing free transportation to and from Washington, D.C., where they visit that city's war memorials. For more information, visit the group's website—http://www.honorflight.org.

Above: Bob Givens during the Honor Flight to Washington, D.C. on May 14, 2011. Three large buses, escorted by squad cars, transported the veterans, who were greeted with a great deal of fanfare, to the impressive World War II Memorial, the Korean Veterans' Memorial, the Iwo Jima Memorial, the Viet Nam Memorial, the Women in Military Service for America Memorial, Arlington National Cemetery, and a distant glimpse of the Pentagon, the Capitol Building, and the White House—all in one day!

Opposite: Exterior and interior views of a restored WWII B-17 that Bob and other Honor Flight attendees visited.

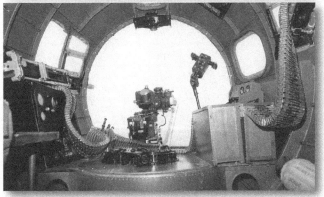

Discussion Questions

1. Who were some of the people that influenced Bob's life, and in what ways did they do so?

2. Who are some of the people that have influenced your life, and in what ways?

3. Bob was bullied more than once as a young man. How did he deal with it? Have you or someone you know ever been bullied? How was it dealt with? What can you do if you witness someone being bullied?

4. Bob did not give up on his goal to join the military. What goal(s) do you have? What people, activities, or preparations can help you reach your goal(s)?

5. What are some of the skills and personal qualities that helped save Bob's life after he fell out of the plane and into the North Sea? Did any of these things help him later in life? In what way did they do so?

6. What qualities or skills do you possess that could potentially save your life? In what way could they do so? How could you learn or obtain other qualities or skills that could help you in a life-threatening situation?

7. At the end of Bob's long life, what did he value most? At this point in your life, what do you value most? Why?

About the Author

S. FABIAN BUTALLA was born and raised in Toledo, Ohio; graduated from Bowling Green State University; taught junior high school English in Oregon, Ohio and Los Angeles California; senior high school English and College Writing at two schools in northern Minnesota; and then served as K-12 Media Director in five schools within the St. Louis County District of northern Minnesota, totaling more than thirty-two years in the field of education. Ms. Butalla currently lives in northern Minnesota.

www.hellgatepress.com